1993

Landmarks of world literature

Byron

DON JUAN

BYRON

Don Juan

ANNE BARTON

Professor of English, University of Cambridge, and Fellow of Trinity College

CAMBRIDGE
UNIVERSITY PRESS

Published by the Press Syndicate of the University of Cambridge
The Pitt Building, Trumpington Street, Cambridge CB2 1RP
40 West 20th Street, New York NY 10011-4211, USA
10 Stamford Road, Oakleigh, Victoria 3166, Australia

First published 1992

Printed in Great Britain by Redwood Press Limited, Melksham, Wiltshire.

A catalogue record for this book is available from the British Library

Library of Congress cataloguing in publication data

Barton, Anne.
Byron, Don Juan / Anne Barton.
    p.   cm. − (Landmarks of world literature)
Includes bibliographical references.
ISBN 0 521 32933 7 (hardback)
1. Byron, George Gordon Byron, Baron, 1788−1824. Don Juan.
2. Don Juan (Legendary character) in literature.   I. Title.
II. Series.
PR4359.B37   1992
821′.7 − dc20   92−5280 CIP

ISBN 0 521 32933 7 hardback

WG

For J.P. Stern

Contents

vii

Preface

The section headings of chapters 1, 2 and 4 in this volume are intended as straightforward descriptions of their contents. The long central chapter (3) offers a chronological reading of *Don Juan*, the quotations from the poem which serve as titles for the nine sections indicating the principal area of concern in each.

Some parts of sections three and four in chapter 3 were originally given as a paper, '*Don Juan* Re-considered: The Haidée Episode', at the conference on *Byron e la Cultura Veneziana* at Mira and Venice in September 1986, and subsequently printed in the proceedings of that conference (Università degli studi di Venezia, edited by Giulio Marra, Angelo Righetti, Anna Rosa Scrittori and Bernard Hickey) and in *The Byron Journal*, 15, 1987. I am grateful to the editors concerned for permission to re-use this material.

I should also like to thank David Woodhouse, who read this book in typescript and, as well as locating some elusive quotations, commented on it helpfully.

The edition of *Don Juan* used in this book (quotations are identified by canto and stanza number) is that prepared by Jerome J. McGann, volume V of *Lord Byron, The Complete Poetical Works*, Clarendon Press, Oxford, 1986. Quotations from Byron's letters and journals (BLJ), giving volume and page number, refer to *Byron's Letters and Journals*, edited by Leslie Marchand, vols. I–XI, John Murray, London, 1973–82.

This was one of the last Landmark volumes edited by Peter Stern. Although gravely and, as he was aware, terminally ill, he read and commented on it with his customary insight and care. The book is much the better for his constructive criticism and suggestions. At that time, he graciously permitted me to dedicate it to him. It is dedicated now, in gratitude and sorrow, to his memory.

Chronology

	Byron's life and works	Important literary events	Important historical events
1788	Birth, in London, on 22 January, of George Gordon Byron. He is born with a club-foot, about which he will remain extremely sensitive all his life	Publication of final volumes of Gibbon's *The Decline and Fall of the Roman Empire*; Goethe's *Egmont*	
1789	Mrs Byron and her son settle in lodgings in Aberdeen	Blake's *Songs of Innocence*	Storming of the Bastille in Paris
1790		Burke's *Reflections on the Revolution in France*	*Fête de la Fédération* in France
1791	Death (possibly by suicide) of John Byron, the poet's father, in France	First part of Paine's *The Rights of Man* (second part published in 1792)	
1792			Unsuccessful denouncement of Robespierre
1793		Godwin's *An Enquiry Concerning Political Justice*	Execution of Louis XVI. War declared between France and England
1794	Byron becomes heir to the peerage, following the death of the grandson of the fifth Lord Byron	Blake's *Songs of Experience*; Paine's *The Age of Reason*; death of Gibbon	Reign of Terror and fall of Robespierre. Treason Trials in London, and suspension of Habeas Corpus
1795			British Government acts to limit all forms of political association and expression

1796	Coleridge publishes *Poems on Various Subjects*	
1798	Publication by Wordsworth and Coleridge of *Lyrical Ballads*; first version of Malthus' *Essay on the Principle of Population*	
1799	Schiller's *Wallenstein's Tod*	Napoleon made First Consul of France for ten years
1800	Death of Cowper	The French defeat Austria and retake Italy
1801	Second edition of *Lyrical Ballads*, with Preface by Wordsworth; Chateaubriand's *Atala*	
1802	Scott's *Border Minstrelsy*; first issue of *The Edinburgh Review*	Peace of Amiens; Napoleon becomes First Consul for life
1803		Renewal of war with France
1804	Schiller's *William Tell*; Wordsworth completes *Ode: Intimations of Immortality*	Napoleon crowns himself Emperor
1805	Chateaubriand's *René*; Scott's *Lay of the Last Minstrel*	Battles of Trafalgar and Austerlitz
1806		
1807	Wordsworth's *Poems in Two Volumes*; Mme de Staël's *Corinne*	

Byron column:

1798	Byron inherits the title after the death of his great-uncle, the fifth Lord Byron. He and his mother visit Newstead Abbey, in Nottinghamshire, the family seat
1799	Byron is sent to Dr Glennie's school in Dulwich to be prepared for Harrow
1800	Byron enters Harrow
1805	Enters Trinity College, Cambridge, and begins to run up serious debts
1806	Has his first volume of poems, *Fugitive Pieces*, privately printed
1807	*Poems on Various Occasions* privately printed, followed a few months later by the public appearance of *Hours of Idleness*. Leaves Cambridge for London and a life of debt and dissipation

	Byron's life and works	Important literary events	Important historical events
1808	*Hours of Idleness* savaged by Henry Brougham in *The Edinburgh Review*	Goethe's *Faust*, Part I	Beginning of the Peninsular War
1809	Takes his seat in the House of Lords. Publishes his first satire, *English Bards and Scotch Reviewers*, and then leaves England with his Cambridge friend, John Cam Hobhouse, to travel in Portugal, Spain, Malta, Greece, Turkey and Albania. Begins *Childe Harold's Pilgrimage*	*Quarterly Review* founded by Scott and Murray	
1810	Byron swims the Hellespont from Sestos to Abydos. Hobhouse returns to England but Byron remains in Greece. He writes the first version of *Hints from Horace*, and also *The Curse of Minerva*, protesting against the removal of the Elgin Marbles	Crabbe's *The Borough*	
1811	Returns to England in July. Death of his mother, his Cambridge friend Matthews, and his Trinity protégé, the choirboy John Edleston	Austen's *Sense and Sensibility*	Prince of Wales becomes Regent
1812	Delivers his maiden speech (on the Frame-breaking Bill) in the House of Lords. Thinks of leaving England again and settling in the East. *Childe Harold*, published in March, is a huge success.		Beginning of the French retreat from Moscow

	Second speech in the House of Lords (Catholic Claims Bill). Affairs with Lady Caroline Lamb and Lady Oxford. Proposes to Annabella Milbanke, and is rejected		
1813	Publishes the first of his Eastern tales, *The Giaour*. It goes through a number of editions. Third and last speech in the House of Lords. Affair with his half-sister, Augusta Leigh. Begins a Journal, publishes *The Bride of Abydos* and begins *The Corsair*	Shelley's *Queen Mab*; Austen's *Pride and Prejudice*	Battle of Leipzig
1814	*The Corsair* sells 10,000 copies on the first day of publication. Proposes a second time to Annabella Milbanke, and is accepted. Writes and publishes *Lara*	Austen's *Mansfield Park*; Scott's *Waverley*; Wordsworth's *The Excursion*	Napoleon abdicates; First Treaty of Paris; Congress of Vienna
1815	Marries Annabella, in January, at a private ceremony in her parents' house in Yorkshire. Publication of *Hebrew Melodies*. Byron joins the sub-committee of management of Drury Lane Theatre. His daughter, Augusta Ada, is born in December. His creditors become pressing	Wordsworth's *The White Doe of Rylstone* and collected edition of *Poems*	Napoleon's return from Elba; Battle of Waterloo; Restoration of the Bourbons; Second Treaty of Paris; Napoleon exiled to St Helena
1816	Lady Byron and Ada leave London for her parents' home, and Byron eventually agrees to a legal separation.	Coleridge's *Christabel and Other Poems*; Constant's *Adolphe*; Austen's *Emma*; Lady Caroline Lamb's	Spa Fields riots in London; Depression and discontent

	Byron's life and works	Important literary events	Important historical events
	Publication of *The Siege of Corinth* and *Parasina*. Affair with Claire Clairemont. In April, after being snubbed at Lady Jersey's party, he leaves England, never to return. Travels through Belgium, visits the field of Waterloo, and begins a third canto of *Childe Harold*. Settles in the Villa Diodati, near Geneva, and becomes friendly with Shelley, who lives nearby. Writes *The Prisoner of Chillon*. In the autumn, Byron and Hobhouse set off on a tour of Italy, and Byron settles in Venice. Affair with Marianna Segati. Third canto of *Childe Harold* published	*Glenarvon*; Scott's *Old Mortality*; Goethe's *Italienische Reise*	
1817	Allegra, his daughter by Claire Clairemont, is born in England. Byron finishes his drama, *Manfred*. In April, he travels to Rome, returning to Venice at the end of May. Begins Canto IV of *Childe Harold* in June. Affair with Margarita Cogni. Finishes *Beppo* in October	Coleridge's *Biographia Literaria* and *Sybilline Leaves*; *Blackwood's Edinburgh Magazine* started; first two cantos of Frere's *The Monks and the Giants* ('Whistlecraft'); Moore's *Lallah Rooke*; Scott's *Rob Roy*; Keats' *Poems*; death of Austen and de Staël	Serious social unrest in Britain; Death of the Princess Charlotte
1818	*Beppo* published (anonymously) and Canto IV of *Childe Harold*. He begins *Don Juan* in July. Moves into the Palazzo Mocenigo on the Grand Canal.	Publication of Mary Shelley's *Frankenstein*; Keats' *Endymion*; Shelley's *The Revolt of Islam* and *Julian and Maddalo*; Peacock's	Conference of Aix-la-Chapelle; European Alliance

	Byron's life	Literary context	Historical events
	Writes his 'Memoirs'. Reads Canto I of *Don Juan* to Shelley. Begins Canto II in December	*Nightmare Abbey*; Scott's *The Heart of Midlothian*; posthumous publication of Austen's *Northanger Abbey* and *Persuasion*	'Peterloo Massacre' in Manchester
1819	Newstead Abbey is sold. Byron falls in love with the young Countess Guiccioli. Cantos I and II of *Don Juan* published (anonymously) in July. Byron follows the Countess Guiccioli to Ravenna. He gives his 'Memoirs' to Thomas Moore. Finishes Cantos III and IV of *Don Juan* in November	Shelley's *The Cenci*; Crabbe's *Tales of the Hall*; Wordsworth's *Peter Bell* and *The Waggoner*	
1820	Settles in Ravenna. Translates first canto of Pulci's *Morgante Maggiore*. Involvement with the Italian Carbonari movement. Writes his first neo-classical tragedy, *Marino Faliero*. The Pope agrees to the separation of the Countess Guiccioli and her husband. Byron finishes Canto V of *Don Juan* in November	Keats' *Lamia and Other Poems*; Shelley's *Prometheus Unbound*; Clare's *Poems Descriptive of Rural Life and Scenery*; Lamartine's *Méditations poétiques*	Death of George III; Accession of George IV; Trial of Queen Caroline; Cato Street Conspiracy; Royalist reaction in Europe; Revolution in Spain and Portugal
1821	Begins his 'Ravenna Journal'. Writes *Sardanapalus*. *Marino Faliero* performed at Drury Lane, despite Byron's objections. Tells Murray he has decided, at the Countess Guiccioli's request, to abandon *Don Juan*. Writes *The Two Foscari* and the biblical drama *Cain*. Cantos III–V of *Don Juan* are	De Quincey's *Confessions of an English Opium Eater*; Southey's *A Vision of Judgement*; Goethe's *Wilhelm Meisters Wanderjahre*; H. von Kleist's *Der Prinz von Homburg*; Shelley's *Defence of Poetry*, *Epipsychidion* and *Adonais*; Clare's *The Village Minstrel*; death of Keats	Death of Napoleon; Greek War of Independence begins; Death of Queen Caroline

	Byron's life and works	Important literary events	Important historical events
1821	published in August. Writes *Heaven and Earth* and *The Vision of Judgement*. Begins another journal, 'Detached Thoughts'. He and the countess and her family join the Shelleys in Pisa. Byron meets Captain Medwin, who keeps a record of his conversation		
1822	Byron finishes *Werner*, begins *The Deformed Transformed*, and also secretly resumes work on *Don Juan* in January. In April, his daughter Allegra dies of a fever. Shelley is drowned in the Bay of Spezia. By the end of August, Byron has written nearly four more cantos of *Don Juan*. He moves to Genoa with the Guiccioli family in September, where he finishes Canto X. *The Vision of Judgement* is published anonymously in *The Liberal*. Cantos XI and XII of *Don Juan* are finished by December	Heine's *Gedichte*; Hunt starts *The Liberal*; death of Shelley; Stendhal's *De l'Amour*	Suicide of Castlereagh
1823	Writes *The Island*, his last verse tale. Finishes Canto XIII of *Don Juan* in February, and XIV and XV in March. Meets the countess of Blessington in April, who records his conversation.	Stendhal's *Racine et Shakespeare*; Lamb's *Essays of Elia* published as a book; Scott's *Quentin Durward*	Agricultural discontent; War between France and Spain

Finishes Canto XVI of *Don Juan* in May and begins XVII. John Hunt publishes Cantos VI–VIII in July after Byron has broken off publishing relations with Murray. Byron receives a message from The Greek Committee in London, decides to go to Greece, and arrives in Cephalonia in August. Hunt publishes Cantos IX–XI of *Don Juan* in this month, and XII–XIV in December

1824 Byron goes to Missolonghi in January, and prepares for active operations. Writes 'On this Day I Complete my Thirty-Sixth Year'. Hunt publishes Cantos XV–XVI of *Don Juan*. On 9 April, Byron is caught in heavy rain while out riding, becomes feverish, then gravely ill, and dies on Easter Monday, 19 April. The body is embalmed and shipped back to England. In May, his 'Memoirs' are burned. The fragment of *Don Juan*, Canto XVII, found among Byron's papers after his death, is first published in 1907

Chapter 1

The making of *Don Juan*

George Gordon, sixth Lord Byron, began *Don Juan*, a work meant initially 'to be a little quietly facetious upon every thing' (BLJ VI. 67), in Venice on 3 July 1818. By the following January, he had completed two out of what, at this time, he envisaged as twelve cantos of a substantial stanzaic poem, and was embroiled in fierce debate with his friends back in England, all of whom begged him either to make drastic cuts or (better still) not to publish at all. Byron, however, was unpersuadable. Cantos I and II appeared in the summer of 1819, without either the author's or publisher's name on the title page, stripped of the Dedication, and (to the author's fury) with asterisks replacing some lines and stanzas, but otherwise intact. The reception of these cantos in England was exactly what had been feared. Byron's authorship, proclaimed equally by the wit and brilliance of the poem and by what most readers felt to be its blasphemy, immorality and outrageous satire on contemporaries, including the poet's estranged wife, was clear from the start. A 'filthy and impious poem' was the verdict of *Blackwood's Magazine* in August 1819; an 'infamous publication' that 'will do more harm to the English character than anything of our time' the response of William Wordsworth. Even the courtesan Harriette Wilson professed to be shocked: 'Dear *Adorable* Lord Byron, *don't* make a mere *coarse* old libertine of yourself.' Byron, meanwhile, in his self-imposed Italian exile, came to take *Don Juan* more and more seriously, as 'a *satire* on *abuses* of the present *states* of Society – and not an eulogy of vice' (BLJ X. 68). Stubbornly he continued to write, and at intervals to publish, further cantos of what Shelley was for a long time alone in recognizing as a landmark: the greatest long poem in English since *Paradise Lost*.

Shelley never read Wordsworth's *Prelude*, the one post-Miltonic work which might have challenged *Don Juan* in his estimation. Nervously aware of the extent to which this poem 'on his own life' was private and self-absorbed, Wordsworth reserved it for posthumous publication, by which time both Shelley and Byron were dead. *Don Juan* too is intensely personal: 'Almost all *Don Juan* is *real* life', Byron maintained, 'either my own, or from people I know' (BLJ VIII. 186). Biography, the circumstances and events of the author's past, his loves, hates, sexual relationships, friendships, journeys and opinions, is integral to it, constantly forcing the reader to remember the facts of Byron's short but crowded existence. It is not, however, a private poem in the manner of *The Prelude*. When Byron said of it defensively, 'it may be profligate – but is it not *life*, is it not *the thing*? – Could any man have written it – who has not lived in the world?' (BLJ VI. 232), the world he had in mind encompassed most of Europe. What he chiefly disliked about Wordsworth and his circle (apart from their turncoat politics and disdain for the Augustan poets) was a narrowness and provinciality radically opposed to his own cosmopolitanism: their preference, as he complained in the Dedication of *Don Juan*, for each other's company to the exclusion of wider acquaintance, and for Cumberland lakes over his own global ocean. *Don Juan* has been called, with some justice, the epic of modern life. It is a consciously perverse epic: digressive, largely unplanned and accretive, left unfinished in 1824 at the beginning of Canto XVII, when Byron died at the age of thirty-seven in the Greek War of Independence. A picaresque adventure story interwoven with the meditations and recollections of a compelling, highly individual narrator, the poem is at once the most gloriously comic and the saddest of tales. It also reflects an entire era of European social, political and intellectual history as perceived by a man who had lived both more intensely and more variously, in and out of England, than almost any of his contemporaries.

Byron and the Don Juan tradition

Like so much else in the poem, Byron's choice of hero was mischievous. The narrator informs readers at the outset that he has selected 'our ancient friend Don Juan' (I. 1) only because an epic needs a hero and neither the England of George III, the French Revolution, nor the Napoleonic Wars offer a suitable contemporary figure. Of the many previous treatments of Don Juan, Byron (a frequent opera-goer) certainly knew Mozart's *Don Giovanni*, and probably more than one of the plays written about the Don since his original appearance in Tirso da Molina's *El Burlador de Sevilla* (1630). He mentions, however, only those pantomime versions of the story, popular in early nineteenth-century London, in which the seducer, with the approval of all right-thinking people, is 'sent to the devil, somewhat ere his time' (I. 1). Improvisational, topical, eclectic and transformative, Byron's poem has, as Peter Graham argues, a certain amount in common both with Italian *commedia dell'arte* and with English spectacular theatre, including pantomime, in its various forms.

In establishing this fictional Spanish libertine, murderer and blasphemer as the hero of his poem, Byron clearly intended to tease the prigs. He perplexed them further by presenting a Don Juan who is gentle, tender-hearted and, although amorous, forever being seduced by women rather than seducing, with none of the traits of his treacherous archetype. The story, moreover, through which Byron conducts him, bears little resemblance to the one handed down by Tirso da Molina. The traditional Don was, and remained, a demonic sensualist, deceiving women of all classes either with false promises of marriage or by pretending, under cover of darkness, to be someone else. His fatal mistake, committed in a moment of bravado, was to invite the statue of a man he murdered, the father of one of his victims, to dinner. The statue obliges, and ends by carrying Don Juan off to Hell.

Byron's Juan, like Tirso's, is born in Seville, but he is the child of an unhappy marriage transparently based on Byron's own. After hounding her unfortunate husband to death, the learned and hypocritical Donna Inez brings up her only child according to the strictest moral principles, protecting him carefully from any fact that 'hints continuation of the species' (I. 40). In consequence, Juan finds himself, at sixteen, committing adultery with Donna Julia, a young woman saddled with an elderly husband, without in the least understanding how he has arrived in her bed. Discovery precipitates a divorce, and Juan is packed off to travel until the scandal has died down (Canto I). His ship sinks in mid-ocean. After surviving agonies of hunger and thirst in a crowded open boat where men are driven to eat each other, Juan is washed ashore on a remote Greek island, the sole survivor. Rescued by Haidée, only daughter of the island's pirate owner, he enjoys for a few months the one perfect love relationship of his life — an idyll destroyed by the sudden return of Haidée's father, who sells him into slavery (Cantos II–IV). In Constantinople, Juan catches the eye of the sultan's favourite wife, who buys him and has him smuggled into the harem in women's clothes. Still grieving for Haidée, Juan resists the advances of the sultana, only to give way that night to the voluptuous charms of the harem girl Dudù (Cantos V–VI). After a narrow escape, he finds himself involved as a mercenary soldier in the sack of the Turkish city Ismail by Russian forces (Cantos VII–VIII). Despatched to bring news of this ghastly victory to the Empress Catherine, Juan becomes her 'man-mistress' and subsequently, when his health begins to suffer, is sent on a diplomatic mission to England (Cantos IX–X). When the poem breaks off (Canto XVII), Juan has endured a London 'season', has just been seduced by a frolicsome duchess at a country house party during the Parliamentary recess, and is hovering on the brink of a far more dangerous entanglement with Lady Adeline, his hostess.

Although Byron sometimes toyed with the idea of a conclusion recounting 'Juan's last elopement with the devil' (I. 203), particularly in the early stages of the poem's composition, it is difficult to see how Juan's story as he tells it could be made to accommodate the traditional catastrophe in any but a metaphorical sense. When Byron assured his readers in Canto I that

'a panorama view of hell's in training, / After the style of
Virgil and of Homer' (I.200), he had in mind a parody of
classical epic at least as much as a dig at orthodox Christian
ideas of eternal damnation. But he had not foreseen the direction his poem was to take in its last six cantos, where mock-epic
gives way to a detailed, almost novelistic social realism. Byron
was not entirely in jest when he told his publisher, Murray,
on 16 February 1821 that he was undecided whether to make
his hero 'end in Hell, or in an unhappy marriage, not knowing
which would be the severest. The Spanish tradition says Hell:
but it is probably only an Allegory of the other state' (BLJ
VIII.78). At the same time he made it clear that the agent of
Juan's death was not to be any avenging statue, but the knife of
the guillotine: he was to fall victim, in Paris, to Robespierre's
Terror.

In the event, Byron's own death left Juan permanently
suspended over breakfast at Norman Abbey, the object of
attention from three very different women, with his immediate,
let alone his long-term, future still unclear. Adultery with Lady
Adeline resulting (again) in a divorce seems inevitable, as does
marriage to the coolly reflective Catholic heiress, Aurora Raby,
whose partial resemblance to Lady Byron already augurs ill.
After that, a possible flight from domestic misery straight into
the French Revolution or, also possible, a whole series of intervening foreign adventures, in Germany and Italy, depending on
whether Byron was to be trusted when he said he now aimed at
the traditional epic total of twenty-four cantos – or when he
proposed, outrageously, 'to canter gently through a hundred'
(XII.55). A number of writers have attempted to finish *Don
Juan*. None has succeeded, for the simple reason that while
further adventures for Juan are relatively easy to imagine, no
one can re-create Byron's narrative voice.

Byron as narrator

It was part of his flouting of tradition that Byron should
deprive his hero of the comic servant – Catalinon, Sganarelle,
or Leporello – who accompanies Don Juan in Tirso, Molière,

Mozart, and all other versions except Byron's own: realistic, fretful, an apprehensive commentator haunted by those moral considerations his master has loftily put aside. In a sense, however, this role has been pre-empted in *Don Juan* by the poem's narrator, with whom it becomes enormously more complex. Byron initially struggled against the idea of narrating the poem in his own person. Although his incorrigible and lifelong habit of inserting new material at the proof stage, or even, in some cases, after publication, helps to obscure the situation, he started out determined to fictionalize the teller of this tale. The narrator is the same rather bumbling Spanish gentleman described in the prose Preface, retailing his story 'in a village in the Sierra Morena on the road between Monasterio and Seville – sitting at the door of a posada with the curate of the hamlet on his right hand, a segar in his mouth, a jug of Malaga or perhaps "right sherris" before him on a small table containing the relics of an olla podrida – the time sunset'. A lifelong bachelor and busybody, inexperienced and shy with women, this narrator claims personal acquaintance in Canto I with Juan and his family, asserts that he actually saw him carried off by the devil, and even admits to once having had 'a pail of housemaid's water' (I. 24) emptied over his head by the young scamp when he tried, officiously, to call.

In the Preface, written probably in the autumn of 1818, Byron uses this figure, wickedly, to parody Wordsworth's note to 'The Thorn' in which the older poet had solemnly advised readers to imagine his narrator as 'a captain of a small trading vessel ... who being past the middle age of life had retired upon an annuity or small independent income to some village or country town of which he was not a native'. Byron ultimately abandoned the Preface without completing it, perhaps because he recognized that his verse Dedication to Robert Southey contained a far more devastating attack on Wordsworth and the Lake poets, and should stand alone. Apart, however, from being hilarious, the rejected prose introduction to *Don Juan* is important for what it reveals about Byron's difficulty in sustaining a narrative voice no one could possibly confuse with that of the author of the poem.

'The reader', he announces, 'is requested to extend his supposed powers of supposing so far as to conceive that the Dedication to Mr. Southey, and several stanzas of the poem itself, are interpolated by the English editor.' This 'English editor' is reminiscent of John Hookham Frere's 'Squire Humphry Bamberham' in *Whistlecraft*, one of Byron's models, the purported source of learning and 'superior reading' beyond the capacity of Frere's artisan narrator. Behind the joke, however, lies Byron's anxious recognition not only that the savagely brilliant Dedication is inconceivable as the work of the anonymous Spanish gentleman, but also that within the poem itself this narrative persona is impossibly constricting, limiting his range and freedom of expression. The 'English editor' provides a rather lame excuse for what is already happening all the time in Canto I: the flashing out of Byron's own, unmistakable voice and personality.

By stanza 82 (of 222) the Spanish gentleman has faded away, never (apart from the teasingly ambiguous stanza 165 in Canto II) to reappear. From then on, the narrator of this 'versified Aurora Borealis' (VII.2) is undisguisedly Byron himself: the master of an infinite variety of moods and vocal tones, in one moment serious, flippant in the next, self-mocking, nostalgic, trying out and discarding poses, playing with the reader, interrogative, sometimes indignant, sceptical and increasingly obsessed with a personal, which is also a historical, past. Only rarely (in three stanzas during the shipwreck, and once at Norman Abbey) does he pretend to be present at the events he describes in any capacity other than that of their creator. He does, however, project aspects of himself onto a dazzling variety of characters, both male and female. To one, the Englishman Johnson, he even lends for a time his own narrative voice. The unity of *Don Juan*, apparently the most wayward and formless of poems, is fundamentally, as has long been recognized, that of Byron's own extraordinary personality. Of consuming interest to contemporaries, both European and English – it has been said that only Byron could have visited the field of Waterloo in 1816, one year after the battle, and generated almost as much interest as the event itself – that personality continues, in his greatest poem, to exert its magnetic pull.

The historical setting

Among Juan's various adventures, only one has a fixed, historical date. The sack of Ismail, an episode in the Russo-Turkish wars, occurred in 1790. Although Byron's mock epic pretensions had involved 'a little touch at warfare' (VI. 120) from the beginning, he almost certainly did not know at the outset that this particular atrocity was the one he was going to select. That decision seems to have been taken when he returned to *Don Juan* in January 1822, after a break of over a year during which the prohibition of his *inamorata*, the Countess Guiccioli (or so he pretended), had put a halt to its progress. Canto VI is a turning-point in the poem, not only because from this point on it would be published by John Hunt rather than by the conservative and increasingly reluctant Murray, but also because here Byron decided 'to throw away the scabbard' (BLJ IX. 191): to attack 'cant' of all kinds – social, political, religious and sexual – regardless of the consequences for his reputation in an England already drifting, particularly among her ruling classes, towards some of the attitudes of the Victorian age. As Jerome McGann has demonstrated, it was in this middle section of *Don Juan* that Byron imposed a retrospective historical time upon the events of the poem as a whole, one distinct from the past and present of the man writing it. If Juan is sixteen at the sack of Ismail in 1790, then he must have been born in 1774 and have left Seville just at the outbreak of the French Revolution. He will die in Paris in 1793 when the Revolution has degenerated into a blood-bath, but before the rise of Napoleon. Byron as narrator, on the other hand, born in 1788, is looking back from the vantage-point of the 1820s not only over the Revolution he was too young to experience himself, but also over the Napoleonic era of his own maturity and fame, and its aftermath of European restoration and reaction: that period of the Holy Alliance, the return of the Bourbon kings, and political unrest, not only in Italy, Spain,

Portugal and Greece, but also in England itself, which his hero would not live to see, but against the background of which *Don Juan* itself was written.

Byron had always, from an early age, been politically engaged. While an undergraduate at Cambridge, he joined the Whig Club, and to this Opposition party in Parliament he remained loyal all his life. When, after the publication in 1812 of Cantos I and II of *Childe Harold*, his versified travel diary, he awoke one morning (as he said) to find himself famous, literary success, combined with youth, brilliance and an apparently devastating physical beauty, opened the doors of all the great Whig houses to this previously obscure and impoverished half-Scottish nobleman. Byron was later to draw on his memories of these years of social celebrity (abruptly terminated by the scandal surrounding the dissolution of his marriage in 1816) for the English cantos of *Don Juan*. Yet he was never entirely comfortable within the Whig party, nor the party with him.

Time has vindicated Byron's three speeches in the House of Lords: against the death penalty as a solution to industrial unrest among the Nottingham weavers; in favour of Catholic emancipation; and for the liberation of an imprisoned proponent of the electoral reforms that were to triumph in 1832. At the time, their 'radicalism' made most Whigs (let alone Tories) uneasy. Yet Byron could never quite bring himself into accord with the whole-hearted radicalism on the fringes of the party associated with William Cobbett, Leigh and John Hunt, or even his lifelong friend John Cam Hobhouse. In later life he was to publish with both Hunts, and to support the *Examiner*, Leigh Hunt's liberal journal. He always remained, however, as Leigh Hunt's wife liked witheringly to observe, 'his lordship': a man fiercely proud of his aristocratic lineage and station, and distrustful of anything resembling 'democratic royalty' (XV. 23). 'I wish men to be free', he asserted in *Don Juan*, 'As much from mobs as kings – from you as me', and admitted that he was bound, in consequence, to 'offend all parties' (IX. 25, 26).

Acutely aware of the protean, contradictory nature of his

own personality ('So that I almost think that the same skin / For one without − has two or three within', XVII.11), Byron told Lady Blessington, shortly before he left on his last journey to Greece, that the only two principles to which he was constant were a 'strong love of liberty and a detestation of cant'. Both in his life and in *Don Juan*, these are fixed poles. Like many of his generation, he initially mistook Napoleon for a liberator, the hero who would put the French Revolution back on course, only to be disillusioned when he turned into yet another imperialist oppressor and then allowed himself to be led off tamely to St Helena. Upon Bonaparte's conqueror Wellington, however (or 'Vilainton', as Byron liked to call him, in imitation of the French mispronunciation of his name), the man who 'repaired Legitimacy's crutch' (IX.3), he visited a hatred untempered by that grudging admiration he retained for Napoleon even when enthroned. Wellington and Castlereagh, the Tory Foreign Minister who helped keep Italy in foreign bondage, victimized the Catholics in Ireland and opposed poor relief at home, were unimaginative agents of tyranny at whom Byron was always too angry to laugh in the way he laughed at the Lake poets, or even at George III, England's mad old king, and later at his corpulent successor.

Although he detested war ('a brain-spattering, windpipe-slitting art', IX.4) in general, and the cult of military glory in particular, Byron made an exception for wars fought in the cause of freedom − in Britain's American colonies, in South America, or in Greece. Convinced that 'Revolution / Alone can save the Earth from Hell's pollution' (VIII.51), he involved himself closely in the abortive Italian Carbonari movement, hiding their arms in his house in Ravenna. Before casting in his lot with the insurgent Greeks, he contemplated going to live in Venezuela, or even returning to England in the event of a political uprising there. Reactionary governments, including that of his native land, had reason to regard not only what he wrote, but also what he might do, with apprehension.

Although Byron took the last, unfinished canto of *Don Juan* with him to Greece in July 1823, he did not work on the poem during the nine months he spent there before his death.

He was occupied during this time trying patiently to sort out
the confused affairs of the country, but it had also always
been characteristic of him to regard his art as an alternative
to action, not its companion. 'Poetry', he said once, 'is the
dream of my sleeping Passions — when they are awake — I
cannot speak their language — only in their Somnambulism'
(BLJ V. 157). In general, the 'Passions' most likely to produce
this effect were political. Eros and poetry were by no means
Byronic incompatibles, as witness the succession of verse tales
which in 1812 and 1813 had helped relieve the tensions of a
whole series of highly emotional affairs, including incest with
his half-sister Augusta. In Greece, most of the little poetry he
did write was forced out of him by an unrequited passion
for the boy Loukas Chalandrutsanos. Politics, however, were
another matter. 'And now let us be literary', he wrote to Moore
in 1821, after the failure of the Italian uprising, 'a sad falling
off, but it is always a consolation. If "Othello's occupation
be gone", let us take to the next best; and if we cannot con-
tribute to make mankind more free and wise, we may amuse
ourselves and those who like it' (BLJ VIII. 104—5). To one of
his companions in Greece, who reproached him for ceasing to
write, he retorted: 'Poetry should only occupy the idle. In more
serious affairs it would be ridiculous.'

   This privileging of action over art, although a standard view
throughout most of human history, ran counter (as Byron was
well aware) to the new Romantic exaltation of the imagination
and its products. It augmented his distrust of Wordsworth,
Coleridge, Keats and other contemporary poets, as well as
driving him to validate his own fictions by way of a substantial
ballast of verifiable fact. Where his own experience (or 'that
of people I know') was unable to supply this, he turned to
documentary accounts. In *Don Juan*, the nautical details of
the shipwreck, the military manœuvres leading to the surrender
and sack of Ismail, the description of the harem at Constantinople or the court of the Empress Catherine, are all based —
as Byron was touchingly eager to make known — upon real,
circumstantial accounts. The shipwreck, for instance, draws
(*inter alia*) upon Dalyell's *Shipwrecks and Disasters at Sea*

(1812), accounts of the wreck of the French frigate *Meduse* in 1816, Bligh's story of the mutiny on the Bounty, and the narrative of his own seafaring grandfather, 'Foulweather Jack'.

The incorporation of factual material into his verse had always been of great importance to Byron. Despite such attempts to justify his art, his life was marked by periodic attempts to wean himself away from poetry altogether. Although morbidly sensitive to criticism, no one could be more scathing and dismissive of his past work and its popularity than Byron himself in certain moods. *Don Juan*, however, became something different: a poem written in the teeth of opposition, with which he had lived, on and off, for five years and had gradually come to value and respect. He put it away in Greece, but it was by no means unrelated to the purposes of that expedition:

> For words are things, and a small drop of ink,
> Falling like dew upon a thought, produces
> That which makes thousands, perhaps millions, think.

(III. 88)

Chapter 2

Style and form

The Italian influence

All of *Don Juan* was written in Italy: in Venice or in Byron's summer villa on the Brenta, then subsequently in Ravenna, Pisa and the outskirts of Genoa, as Byron shifted his residence in accordance with the movements of the Countess Guiccioli and her family. Yet almost none of Byron's actual life in Italy – the libertine excesses of his time in Venice before he met Teresa, his political commitments, the papal decree that finally separated the countess from her husband while leaving her and her liberally inclined father and brother under police surveillance – figures in the poem. The one conspicuous exception is the fate of the military commandant of Ravenna, shot dead outside Byron's house on 9 December 1820, which he describes in Canto V. Whatever Byron's plans for future cantos, Juan himself never reached Italy to become (like Byron himself) *cavalier servente* to another man's wife. With the single exception of Russia, where Byron had never been, the countries traversed by the poem – Spain, Greece, Turkey and England – like that complex personal past upon which the narrator meditates so obsessively, were places experienced 'long ere I dreamt of dating from the Brenta' (I. 212).

Byron had already immortalized his 1817 spring journey through Italy from Venice to Rome in Canto IV of *Childe Harold*. In the autumn of that year he based *Beppo*, sub-titled *A Venetian Story*, on an anecdote supplied by the complaisant husband of his current mistress, Marianna Segati. Like Byron's wonderful Venetian letters of the same period, *Beppo* portrays life in this 'fairy city of the heart' – or 'Sea-Sodom' as Byron called it in his darker moods – life as it was actually lived, not merely observed, by an English poet who spoke fluent Italian and had made himself welcome in Venetian society at all levels: in the salons of the aristocracy, middle-class homes and shops, in the company of artisans, gondoliers, peasant girls and whores. Almost all the English writers who settled for a time in Shelley's 'paradise of exiles, Italy' – Shelley himself, Keats, Browning, Dickens, D.H. Lawrence – remained foreigners. Byron did not. Even the tolerant Shelley, indeed, expressed dismay at finding him, in Venice, so 'thoroughly Italianate'.

Beppo, unlike *Don Juan*, is as much about Byron's life in Venice as it is about Laura, her lover the count, and the 'dead' husband who chooses the carnival as the occasion of his embarrassing return. It is also the poem which made *Don Juan* possible. Byron wrote *Beppo*, as he was the first to admit, in imitation of John Hookham Frere's *Whistlecraft*, itself an adaptation of the *Morgante Maggiore* (1485) by the fifteenth-century Florentine, Luigi Pulci. The copy of *Whistlecraft* that reached Venice in September 1817 impelled Byron almost at once to experiment, like Frere, with *ottava rima* in English. He had long been familiar with the greatest of Italian poems in octave rhyme, Ariosto's *Orlando Furioso* (1516), and probably with Francesco Berni's *Rifacimento* (1541), the 're-making' of Boiardo's earlier *Orlando Innamorato* (1495) which Ariosto's masterpiece had triggered off. In 1816, a gift copy of Giambattista Casti's *Novelle Galanti*, first published in 1790, had reminded him that this style was not necessarily the vehicle for romance, but could be put to contemporary and satiric use. Although Frere was immediately responsible for *Beppo*, Byron soon recognized that he was working in a form, kept alive by modern writers like Casti, that was also of great antiquity: 'as old as the hills in Italy' (BLJ VIII. 229) he later claimed. By February 1820, he had both tracked it back to Pulci ('the parent not only of *Whistlecraft* – but of all jocose Italian poetry', BLJ VII. 42) and had himself just finished a meticulous translation of the first canto of the *Morgante Maggiore*, a labour of love engaging him simultaneously with Cantos III and IV of *Don Juan*, his own epic in *ottava rima*.

Byron and *ottava rima*

Childe Harold, Byron's other long poem, written in two distinct
stages during 1809–10 and 1816–17, had been in Spenserian
stanzas. The first canto's sporadic lunges at archaic diction
('whilome', 'wight', 'ne', 'mote') partly explain the young
Byron's choice of Spenserian form: he was relying on imitative
Elizabethanism to distance both the poem's hero and its narrator
from his recognizable contemporary self. The attempt failed,
and with it the diction, leaving Byron committed to an intricate
stanzaic form with which, even in Cantos I and II, he seems
temperamentally less than comfortable. In the verse tales
produced between 1812 and his resumption of *Childe Harold*
in 1816, he found freedom in the headlong and more congenial
rush of couplets. The return to *Childe Harold* necessitated a
return to the Spenserian stanza, but the more mature and
confident Byron took now to handling it in ways that were a
virtual contradiction of the form.

The nine-line Spenserian unit (ababbcbcc) is a 'stanza' in
the sense of being, as the word indicates, a little 'room', a
self-contained enclosure. Its long last line, an alexandrine,
imposes finality upon the eight decasyllabic lines which precede
it while, at the same time, pointing back by way of the shared
c rhyme to the middle of the stanza and the temporary resting-
point of the b couplet there. The effect is to establish the
stanzas as discrete units, each one representing a fresh start.
The reader is impelled forward less by the formal properties of
the poem, which if anything act as a brake, than by syntax
(connectives like 'as', 'but', 'so' or 'which' frequently beginning
the sentence which launches the next stanza), and by narrative
impetus.

Byron was almost never happy working in small, compressed
verbal units. A master of 'the negligently grand', his lyrics
rarely show him at his best. Even in the early cantos of *Childe
Harold*, the temptation to allow a most un-Spenserian enjamb-
ment between stanzas, a single sentence pouring across the
barrier of the alexandrine into the next unit, sometimes overcame him. By Canto IV, the practice had become endemic,

often linking as many as three stanzas in the same long-breathed flow of verse. The special quality of this concluding canto derives in part from the opposition set up between its essentially centripetal Spenserian stanzas and the onward rush of Byron's thought as the poem cascades over all formal obstacles towards its ultimate destination: the Mediterranean sea. The effect is extraordinary, but it also serves to indicate why in 1817 Byron should have been so eager to exchange the constriction of Spenserian stanzaic form for the relative liberty of *ottava rima*.

The Italian form Byron tried out in *Beppo* and subsequently used for *Don Juan*, eight decasyllabic lines rhyming abababcc, had always been associated with loosely woven narrative poetry: digressive, various in mood, sometimes comic, sometimes grave and frequently conversational in manner. The couplet concluding each verse unit, lacking Spenserian finality, could extend itself naturally into the next stanza, or not, according to the whim of the writer. 'The Soul of such writing is it's [*sic*] licence', Byron commented with obvious delight (BLJ VI. 208). Although taxing, especially in English, in its demand for three a and three b rhymes in each stanza, the mock-epic in *ottava rima* was essentially a relaxed mode. Not only could it be made to accommodate almost anything in the way of material and tone; it was also given to commenting on itself, inviting games with its own formal structure of a kind that Byron found irresistible.

Initially, his greatest problem lay in adapting a vehicle designed for the Italian language to the peculiarities and demands of English. *Beppo*, a *jeu d'esprit* of 792 lines, had been instructive. The manuscripts of *Don Juan*, however, suggest that Byron was still experimenting in the early cantos with his new form, particularly its rhymes. English has fewer rhyme words than Italian. It is also as strongly biased towards masculine rhyme as Italian, with its preponderance of words ending in an articulated vowel, is towards feminine. Most rhymes in Italian are of two syllables, but even three-syllable rhymes rarely seem unusual or forced. In English, by contrast, double rhymes can be, and triple ones frequently are, comic in effect. This is especially so if they comprise more than one word.

In *Whistlecraft*, Frere had deliberately sought out risible combinations ('Parnassus/surpass us', 'Roman/no man') while at the same time increasing the colloquialism and informality of his Italian model. Byron, however, learned to take inventive liberties with his rhymes far in excess of Frere's.

Comic rhymes

Byron began by compelling readers to anglicize the pronunciation of his hero's Spanish name, rhyming it at the outset with 'new one' or 'true one'. Apart from its metrical inconvenience, he would have been hard put to find any English rhymes for 'Juan' as a monosyllable. Sheer devilry, on the other hand, made him go on to record that 'Don Juan's parents lived beside the river, / A noble stream, and call'd the Guadalquivir' (I. 8), lines which sweep the reader along helplessly into a comic mispronunciation which suddenly renders the river anything but 'noble'. The poem is filled with such ingenious traps, some of them – as becomes especially apparent when read aloud – designed to bring the reader to an abrupt halt while he or she reconsiders how to articulate a particular word in the light of the two (or one, in the case of the concluding couplet) with which it is rhymed. To find 'Indigestion' paired with 'question' amuses; the introduction of 'rest eye on' as the third rhyme (XI. 3) produces temporary dismay, modulating after a telling moment of uncertainty into delight. What is to be made of 'rattles' / 'battles' / 'what else', another show-stopper, apart from its obvious intention to diminish the dignity of the central noun? *Don Juan*'s readers are continually being forced to interrogate a rhyme's imperfection: a casual flaw, or an unsettling Byronic joke with the language and their own assumptions?

Byron has often been accused, most famously by T. S. Eliot, of being imperceptive about the English language: 'he added nothing to [it] ... discovered nothing in the sounds, and developed nothing in the meaning of individual words'. Even the readiness with which much of his work lends itself to translation has been held against him. The rhymes of *Don Juan*, however, are not the creation of a man who was incurious about the nature and capacities of English, or who lacked subtlety and imagination in the way he used his native tongue. Analysis, in this century, of Byron's manuscripts has revealed just how extensively and with what care he revised the poem in the act of writing it, especially the early cantos. He seems to have worked particularly hard on the couplets, which tend to be more epigrammatic (in the eighteenth-century English tradition) than their Italian equivalents. There are, nevertheless, more than enough cancelled or altered lines in the main body of his stanzas, minute verbal substitutions and tightenings, adjustments of syntax and of rhyme, to make it clear that Byron (like many another aristocratic author) was by no means telling the whole truth when he claimed that 'never straining hard to versify, / I rattle on exactly as I'd talk / With any body in a ride or walk' (XV. 19). It is true that the poem is consciously chatty. Again and again, lines which at first seem awkward or unmetrical fall brilliantly into place as soon as they are read aloud. Like its colloquialism, however, the apparent artlessness and spontaneity of *Don Juan*, that almost uncanny delusion the reader still entertains, after more than a century and a half, that Byron's masterpiece is actually being written anew while the pages turn, was the product of consummate art.

Byron's comic rhymes are amusing, occasionally outrageous, and usually purposeful. He uses them to set up 'improper' juxtapositions (e.g., 'gunnery/nunnery', 'intellectual/henpeck'd you all'), jolting the reader out of complacency by insisting that objects or activities conventionally regarded as distinct may, in fact, be related in ways that do not necessarily end with their phonetic similarity. Rhyme in *Don Juan*, especially its couplets, can be mercilessly deflationary. In a poem committed, as Helen Gardner once put it, to 'the salutariness of being undeceived', it became one of Byron's most effective weapons. By pairing 'serious' words with trivial ones (e.g., 'adultery/sultry', 'bottle/Aristotle', 'Pyramus/Semiramis'), he was able to find justification in language itself for his mockery of the solemnities and falsehoods in which society cocoons itself. Even the most intelligent contemporary readers and reviewers expressed shock.

One couplet in particular, from the shipwreck episode, became notorious: 'They grieved for those who perish'd with the cutter, / And also for the biscuit casks and butter' (II. 61). It is not clear at just what point Keats (according to Joseph Severn), reading Cantos I and II on his voyage to Italy, hurled *Don Juan* away in disgust, exclaiming that Byron meant to 'fascenate [*sic*] thousands into extreem [*sic*] obduracy of heart'. The 'cutter/butter' couplet, however, may well have been the catalyst. These, certainly, were the lines with which the scandalized review in the August 1819 issue of *Blackwood's Magazine* rested its case, recoiling with horror from their 'demoniacal laugh'. Hazlitt, bravely defending the couplet in 1830 ('Conversations of James Northcote'), remarked on it as a familiar target of critical abuse. The opprobrium, of course, was something Byron had invited. Initiated at the end of stanza 46, the 'cutter/butter' rhyme passes almost unnoticed on its first appearance, as a neutral piece of description: 'Two casks of biscuit, and a keg of butter, / Were all that could be thrown into the cutter.' Its reversal in stanza 61, by contrast, is explosive. Byron began by writing 'As well as for the biscuit casks and butter', allowing grief for their drowned companions to take a slight but becoming precedence, among the survivors in the longboat, over regret for the lost provisions. He looked at the line again, and changed 'As well as' to read 'And also', insisting upon the absolute equality of the distress occasioned, among men adrift on a cruel sea, by the disappearance of shipmates and of a portion of their scanty victuals. It might be ignoble, but it could scarcely help but be true.

Epic and satire

Hazlitt, in 1830, was attempting to defend Byron against accusations (still audible today) that he had callously mocked human suffering. 'Nobody', Hazlitt declared, 'understood the tragi-comedy of poetry so well ... In real life the most ludicrous incidents border on the most affecting and shocking. How fine that is of the cask of butter in the storm! ... It is the mention of this circumstance that adds a hardened levity and a sort of ghastly horror to the scene. It shows the master-hand — there is such a boldness and sagacity and superiority to ordinary rules in it!' Hazlitt did not summon to Byron's assistance the famous episode in Homer (later singled out by Aldous Huxley in 'Tragedy and the Whole Truth'), in which Odysseus, and those of his men who have escaped the murderous paws of Scylla, prepare an excellent dinner, eat it, and only then permit themselves the luxury of tears for their dead comrades before they sleep. Byron, unlike Homer, laughs at the instinct for self-preservation, but it is a bitter laugh, that of a disappointed idealist exasperated by a society which refused, unlike himself — or Homer — to acknowledge certain uncomfortable facts about human nature.

That Byron relied on the *Odyssey* throughout *Don Juan*, in a fashion more shadowy but nonetheless akin to that of James Joyce in *Ulysses*, has been argued with some plausibility. Not only does he offer his readers frequent tongue-in-cheek assurances that 'my name of Epic's no misnomer' (I. 200), dangling before them the traditional Homeric and Virgilian prospects of love, war, storms at sea, a list of ships and captains, and a visit to the underworld; the adventures through which Juan, an increasingly weary traveller, is made to pass often also evoke specific Odyssean parallels. Homer, and to some extent Virgil, have to be counted, along with Pulci, Berni, Casti and Frere, as shaping literary presences in Byron's poem. They are far from being the only influences, even among writers of the ancient world.

Byron's reading of both classical and modern authors, fiction and non-fiction, was unsystematic but enormous. Those who knew him remarked continually on the retentive and associative nature of his memory; how what he read, passing through 'the glowing alembic of his mind', as Lady Blessington described it, gave rise (often long after) to 'chains of thought, the first idea serving as the original link on which the others were formed'. Almost all *Don Juan* may have been real life, as Byron claimed. His own experience had always been complexly intertwined with the books he read: as a boy, at Harrow and Cambridge, and subsequently almost every day during the remainder of his existence.

Byron provided *Don Juan* with three epigraphs: one presiding over its first two cantos; the second (omitted by Murray) intended to introduce Cantos III and IV; and the third marking the place where the poem divides, at the beginning of Canto VI. The first of these, *Difficile est proprie communia dicere*, is a quotation from Horace: ''Tis no slight task to write on common things', as Byron himself translated it in *Hints From Horace*. His original epigraph, *Domestica facta*, vetoed in proof by Hobhouse as pointing too scandalously towards Byron's marriage, had also been from Horace. (An intervening motto, the evangelical preacher's 'No hopes for them as laughs', was quickly rejected by the poet himself.) Byron confessed in *Childe Harold* how, as a schoolboy, he had hated Horace, that urbane and reasonable practitioner of the plain style in verse: 'not for thy faults, but mine'. Temperamentally he had always been drawn towards the savage invective, the withering contempt, of Rome's other great satirist, Juvenal. His choice of Horace for the initial *Don Juan* epigraph is significant. Juvenalian passion and heightened rhetoric still take over when Byron becomes angry – with Castlereagh in the Dedication, or at Ismail – but the dominant satiric tone, conversational, colloquial, moderate and wryly amused, is Horatian. It was a mode associated for Byron not only with Horace himself, but also with his English followers, those latter-day Augustans he so admired and was increasingly drawn to defend against the disregard or contempt of the other Romantics.

First among Byron's poetic ten commandments, delivered near the end of Canto I and widely deplored as blasphemous, is the injunction: 'Thou shalt believe in Milton, Dryden, Pope' (I. 205). This, in its time, constituted literary as well as religious blasphemy. Of the three names put forward, only Milton's was still venerated by the majority of Byron's literate contemporaries. He was almost alone among the Romantics in his conviction that 'we are upon a wrong revolutionary poetic system', that there was an 'ineffable distance in point of sense – harmony – effect – and even *Imagination* Passion – & *Invention*' between the Augustans (especially Pope) and the writers, himself included, of his own period (BLJ V. 265).

In his early satires *English Bards and Scotch Reviewers* and *Hints From Horace*, Byron had deliberately imitated the couplets and manner of Pope. Pope is still visible as a model in *Don Juan*, despite the *ottava rima* form, but his verbal patterns – orderly, symmetrical, assured – have been Byronized. Fragments of Pope, as Donald Davie memorably puts it, 'gleam, like spars from a shipwrecked world, all about the tumultuous sea of Byron's verse, a criterion acknowledged but no longer to the point'. Pope had passed judgement on knaves and dunces in his satires from the standpoint of an embattled but fixed moral and social order. Byron not only presents a chaotic world, illogical, contradictory and endlessly changing; his own viewpoint and reactions are similarly unstable: 'For me, I know nought; nothing I deny, / Admit, reject, contemn' (XIV. 3).

Although he rummages ceaselessly in *Don Juan* among religions, philosophies and the revelations of contemporary science, the narrator's genuine desire to embrace a system, whether Christian, idealist, moral, or empirical, is continually frustrated by his ingrained scepticism and common sense:

> But still the spouseless Virgin *Knowledge* flies.
>   What are we? and whence came we? what shall be
> Our *ultimate* existence? what's our present?
> Are questions answerless, and yet incessant.
>
> (VI. 63)

Berkeley's denial of the material world's existence may be impossible to confute, a system 'Too subtle for the airiest human head', and yet (kicking the stone like Dr Johnson) 'who can believe it?' (XI. 1). 'So little do we know what we're about in / This world, I doubt if doubt itself be doubting' (IX. 17). Byron, who intended to bring up his daughter Allegra as a Catholic, retained a strongly religious impulse all his life. He remained, however, unable to reconcile human suffering, and that of animals, with the idea of a benevolent Deity. The doctrine of Hell, an eternity of pain, he found particularly repellent. Like his sexual frankness, Byron's honest and uncomfortable – indeed tormented – agnosticism was to wait a long time before it aroused more than isolated and clandestine sympathy in what was generally (if snobbishly) thought to constitute the English reading public. By the 1840s, even Frere was explaining that Byron's use of *ottava rima* in *Don Juan* had made this stanzaic form so opprobrious that he could not possibly be expected now to produce further instalments of *Whistlecraft*.

Chapter 3

The poem

'Fierce loves and faithless wars'

In the opening stanza of *The Faerie Queene*, Spenser promised his readers that 'Fierce warres and faithfull loues shall moralize my song.' Although the narrator of *Don Juan*, surveying his poem from the savageries of Canto VII, pretends not to know whether he is quoting Spenser accurately – 'I am not sure / If this be the right reading' (VII. 8) – Byron's inversion of 'faithful' to 'faithless', and his transposition of the two adjectives, was deliberate. Whatever Spenser – and other epic poets who celebrated martial prowess – liked to imagine, most wars are fought for duplicitous and inglorious reasons. Byron was by no means alone among his contemporaries in finding the traditional warrior ethos of epic, supposedly the noblest of literary forms, distasteful. Nobody, however, wrote anything to equal his unsparing description of the siege of Ismail, that hideous modern Troy. As for 'fierce loves', with everything this implies in its Byronic context about the mutuality of male and female sexual passion and its concurrent destructiveness, that – for many of his original readers – was wholly unacceptable.

In a letter of 8 September 1818, Byron claimed to have slept with more than two hundred women 'of one sort or another' during his first two years in Venice (BLJ VI. 66). On 19 January 1819, writing to Hobhouse and his banker Kinnaird, he constructed a partial list, in imitation of Leporello's famous catalogue in Mozart's *Don Giovanni*, but fleshed out with names (BLJ VI. 92). Even allowing for a measure of exaggeration, it is clear that Byron's libertine excesses during this period, before a combination of ill health and a consuming passion for the young Countess Guiccioli brought them to a halt, recalled the legendary Don Juan's in quantity, although scarcely in character. His own fictional hero, by contrast, stumbles into only five affairs in the course of the entire poem. All five of these erotic entanglements, however, the majority of them initiated by the woman, are ultimately disastrous.

Byron's complex and contradictory attitudes towards the opposite sex are of more than merely biographical interest. In *Don Juan* he brought them all together within the parameters of a single poem, marshalling them into an artistic order, without pretending that in real life they could be reconciled. When young and callow, Byron had complained (BLJ I.161) that his present mistress had 'two faults unpardonable in a woman': she could read and write. Later, he waged comic war against 'bluestockings' and 'chilly women' – and then married one. He claimed to be happiest with passionate 'animals' like the Fornarina, his tempestuous Venetian mistress, remained perpetually blind to the inadequacies of his sister, the feather-brained Augusta, but also maintained close friendships with a series of highly intelligent and perceptive women: Lady Melbourne, Lady Oxford, Madame de Staël, the Countess Benzoni and Lady Blessington. Ungenerous to Keats and the Lake poets, he was full of admiration for the plays of Joanna Baillie. Teresa Guiccioli, his 'last attachment', although a sentimentalist concerned to hand down to posterity a romanti-cized view of her intensely physical affair with Byron, was nevertheless no fool.

While distrusting and sometimes abusing women, Byron was at the same time probably more sensitively cognizant than any other male writer in the period of the waste and futility of so many of their lives, and their unequal treatment by society: commodities reared to be sold in the marriage market, often with nothing awaiting them, whatever their capacity for love, their virtue, beauty and education, but 'A thankless husband, next a faithless lover, / Then dressing, nursing, praying, and all's over' (II.200). 'The gilding', he observed in Canto XIV, 'wears so soon from off [their] fetter' (25). 'Fetter', associated by this point in *Don Juan* with the literal enslavement of women in the harems of the East (where '*Wedlock* and a *Padlock* mean the same', V.158) suddenly throws the whole, supposedly enlightened, basis of English monogamy into question. In suggesting that any woman, questioned at thirty, would honestly rather have been male than female, a schoolboy in preference to a queen (XIV.25), Byron was probably thinking of poor, unhappy Queen Caroline, George IV's wife, deserted by him after one year of marriage, and subsequently the object of grotesque divorce proceedings (on the grounds of suspected adultery with her courier) pressed by a royal husband who not only had several mistresses himself, but also another, common-law, wife. He was also, more generally, deploring the circumscription and injustice of women's lives, even in positions which pretend to give them power.

Alive to 'the real sufferings of their she condition', Byron also knew (and included himself in the indictment) that 'Man's very sympathy with their estate / Has much of selfishness and more suspicion' (XIV.24). That kind of understanding needs to be set against his brazen catalogue of casual, Venetian amours, as does his lifelong susceptibility to the other sex, certain feminine qualities of his own, and a propensity, visible even in childhood, to fall passionately and single-mindedly in love. The same man who callously enumerated his conquests was periodically devastated by the loss, or merely the absence, of a particular woman. Even towards the end of his life, when he was fretting in his role as *cavalier servente* to the Countess Guiccioli, Byron confessed wryly to Hobhouse, when she was forced to leave him briefly, that 'today I burst into tears all alone by myself over a Cistern of Gold fishes – which are not pathetic animals' (BLJ VI.214).

The protagonist of *Don Juan* inherits his creator's susceptibility, his tenderness and inability to say 'No'. Byron's poem begins, with mocking disregard for the classical *medias res*, where no previous version of the Don Juan story had begun, let alone the epic narratives of Homer and Virgil. It examines the damaged childhood and troubled adolescence of its hero. Contemporaries were quick to recognize in Juan's mother, Donna Inez, that 'learned lady' whose 'favourite science was the mathematical' (I.10, 12), a satiric portrait of Lady Byron and, in the poem's account of the break-up of her marriage, a version of the separation proceedings that ended Byron's own. This was scandalous enough, but not the real reason why, as Byron later observed of Cantos I and II, 'Through needles' eyes it easier for the camel is / To pass, than those two cantos into families' (IV. 97). That had to do with something that in *Beppo* had been safely distanced: *Don Juan*'s insistence from the beginning upon the naturalness, in women as well as men, of sexual desire, and upon the unhappy consequences of society's attempts to stifle it, or to regard marriage as its only acceptable outlet.

Morally impeccable, a credit to society, Donna Inez is actually an accomplished hypocrite. A pretend prude, she prevents her son from acquiring any understanding of his own nascent sexuality, not only censoring the classical authors he reads, but even preventing him from seeing the somewhat in-flammatory illustrations in the family missal – which she reserves for her own private use. Ceaselessly vigilant to detect her husband's sexual misdemeanours, she herself has enter-tained a lover. She connives, moreover, in Juan's seduction (aged sixteen) by Donna Julia – the twenty-three-year-old wife of this former lover – in order 'to open Don Alphonso's eyes, / In case he thought his wife too great a prize' (I. 101). When last heard of in the poem, in Canto X, Inez has re-married and is writing to Juan in Moscow, where his undisguised function is that of imperial gigolo, in order to praise both the improvement in his finances and 'the Empress's *maternal* love' (32).

Byron has a good deal of fun with Donna Inez without extending her a shred of sympathy, something which can be said of no other invented character in the poem, with the exception of the semi-fictional Empress Catherine. The case of Julia is very different. Although she also ranks as one of Inez's victims, Julia contributes to her own downfall. The narrator is amused as he notes the progressive stages of her self-deception: from trust in the blessed Virgin's timely aid, to the idea that she owes it to herself to put her virtue on trial, to the final woolly and misplaced confidence in platonic love; but his discerning paraphrase of her thought processes is affectionate. A refusal to confront the true nature of her feelings about either Juan or her ageing husband leads Julia inexorably to that summer bower where, on the fatal sixth of June, 'One hand on Juan's carelessly was thrown, / Quite by mistake — she thought it was her own' (I. 109), and the rest followed as a matter of course. She ends up incarcerated for life in a nunnery: punished less for adultery in itself than for the social sin (which Donna Inez has so cunningly avoided) of being found out.

When the narrator claims that 'love is taught hypocrisy from youth' (I. 72), it is not really of Donna Inez, in whose cool, calculating nature passion plays little part, that he is thinking, but of Julia's gradual education in deceit: the progress of this warm and generous young woman (the narrator places great emphasis on the supposedly torrid Moorish blood she inherits on her mother's side) from genuine, if self-deluded, virtue to the convincingly outraged and tearful wife who up-braids her husband with such eloquence when he breaks in to search her chamber, all the while concealing her slender boy-lover under the bedclothes. Julia's duplicity in this crisis, verbally brilliant and funny though it is, is not a talent she would have needed or wanted to acquire had her marriage been less stultifying, and escape from it so impossible in her society. Her performance almost succeeds — until the unfortunate discovery, not of Juan himself, but merely of his cast-off shoes. After that, Julia's world disintegrates around her and, as it does so, her natural integrity is restored. Her last letter to Juan, 'written upon gilt-edged paper / With a neat crow-quill, rather hard, but new' (I. 198), remembers Pope's 'Elöisa to Abelard' (1717). Julia, however, is unlike Pope's heroine both in that she does not weep, and in the clarity and candour of her recognition that, although the rest of her life will be spent in hopeless yearning for her lost love, she has no further claim on Juan's affections or even, as other people and interests compete for his attention, his memory. He will forget and she will not, because in the world as it is 'Man's love is of his life a thing apart', while being 'woman's whole existence' (I. 194).

'The vast, salt, dread, eternal deep'

Although Shelley succeeded, when they were neighbours in
Switzerland in 1816, in getting him to read Wordsworth with
some enjoyment, Byron could never really accept Wordsworth's
attitudes towards the natural world. Wordsworth persuaded
himself, irritably, that those passages in the third canto
of *Childe Harold* depicting Byron's rush of feeling for the
mountains around Diodati and the lake of Geneva, were all
plagiarized from his own work, and therefore insincere. In fact,
they are unmistakably Byronic: the reactions of a man who
could not find anything benevolent, healing, or instructive in
nature – and suspected people who did of 'cant' – but was
himself alive to the beauty and, more particularly, the energy
of the world around him. As a poet, Byron could not look at
Lake Leman for long without convulsing it in a tempest whose
vitality he sought personally to appropriate and share. The
challenge, for him, was always that of tapping an elemental,
non-human and certainly amoral force: one animating flowers,
but also, and by preference, hurricanes and torrents, avalanches,
and (especially) the sea.

In *Peter Bell the Third* (1819), Shelley seized acutely upon
the sexlessness of Wordsworth's response to the natural world:

> A kind of moral eunuch,
> He touched the hem of Nature's shift,
> Felt faint – and never dared uplift
> The closest, all-concealing tunic.

> (Part IV, stanza 11)

Had Byron been able to read *The Prelude*, Wordsworth's autobiographical description of 'the Growth of a Poet's Mind', it
could only have confirmed his feeling that sexual desire was a
phenomenon persistently and fraudulently omitted from the
older poet's account of human life, whether other people's,
or his own. Byron's reaction to the truth behind the clumsy
Julia and Vaudracour episode in Book IX of the 1805 *Prelude*,
Wordsworth's feeble attempt to incorporate a version of his
youthful affair with Annette Vallon, while suppressing any hint
of association with himself, is easy to imagine. (The winning

sonnet in a *New Statesman* competition earlier this century, when the existence of Wordsworth's illegitimate child at last became public knowledge, is said to have begun, 'Byron! thou shouldst be living at this hour!') When, in *Don Juan*, Byron exposed his adolescent protagonist to all the proper Wordsworthian influences, sending him into a forest to wander 'by the glassy brooks / Thinking unutterable things' (I.90), the result was merely to demonstrate the irrelevance of those landscapes 'where poets find materials for their books' – and he specifically mentions Wordsworth here – to the torments and desires of puberty.

Despatched on his travels by Donna Inez until the scandal of the Julia affair has been forgotten, Juan finds himself confronting nature in its most formless, inhuman and un-Wordsworthian guise: 'the vast, salt, dread, eternal deep' (II. 103). Essentially an inland poet, Wordsworth usually relegated the sea to the periphery of his vision – as in the famous Snowdon passage (*Prelude* Book XIII), or in the dream about another Flood in Book V – or else treated it in a matter-of-fact fashion, as a highway for ships and commerce. Only for a moment, in the aftermath of his brother John's shipwreck and death, did he confront the sea, in the elegiac stanzas on Peele Castle, in all its terrifying alienness: a fluid, untamable, endlessly metamorphosing thing upon whose waves and tides it would be ridiculous to think of projecting human names, as Wordsworth and his family and friends liked to do with Cumberland peaks and crags. Byron, on the other hand, was drawn all his life towards the sea, both literally and as a poet. From the deck of a ship, a sailing yacht, or (better still) as a swimmer, he felt able to associate himself with its power, but always on its own, non-human terms.

The sea which engulfs the *Trinidada*, the ship on which Juan and his tutor and servants embark from Cadiz for Leghorn, is as pitiless and uncaring in the beautiful, blue calm which follows the storm as it was 'when every wave roll'd menacing to fill' the longboat and overwhelm the thirty men (there are no women) huddled inside (II.61). The rainbow, 'airy child of vapour and the sun' (II.92), which spans the sky after they

have been a week adrift, is a reminder of God's covenant in
the Old Testament and the providential arrival on dry land of
Noah's ark. The castaways take it as a good omen but, like the
dark sea over whose surface they float, it signifies nothing at
all. Apart from Juan himself, there will be no survivors. Meanwhile, hunger and thirst break down one of the most fundamental taboos of civilization, while leaving certain random
social decorums ludicrously unimpaired.

Byron was to be much concerned throughout *Don Juan* with
the body's tyranny over the mind, whether in the narrator's
mock account of how his own piety tends to increase with
sickness ('as I suffer from the shocks / Of illness, I grow much
more orthodox', XI. 5), or the predicament of poor Julia who,
'whispering "I will ne'er consent" – consented' (I. 117). Juan,
at the beginning of his voyage, promises to banish everything
from his thoughts except Julia and his heart's anguish over
losing her, but each lurch of the ship renders him humiliatingly
conscious of the greater and more immediate distress of his
stomach. This soliloquy, his first recorded utterance in the
poem, breaks off abruptly as he becomes 'inarticulate with
re[t]ching' (II. 20). Adrift in the longboat, their food and water
gone and no land in sight, most of Juan's companions are
reduced merely to stomachs. First they kill and devour Juan's
dog, and then his tutor. A few important decencies survive.
Juan, who has tried to prevent Julia's letter from being torn
up for the cannibal lottery, refuses to dine on 'his pastor and
his master' (II. 78); a father tenderly nursing his dying child
forgets his own sufferings. The narrator knows that the events
he depicts are horrible, but he also reserves the right to find
some of them grimly comic.

To one reader who objected to 'the quick succession of fun
and gravity', complaining that 'we are never scorched and
drenched at the same time', Byron (through his publisher
Murray) despatched an impatient, and intermittently bawdy,
itemization of physical experiences involving precisely this
combination of sensations, from swimming in the sea at noon
to being boiled alive in oil like St John (BLJ VI. 207). Within
the nightmare of the shipwreck itself, laughter – apart from

'a kind of wild and horrid glee' (II.50) convulsing those passengers and members of the crew who have managed to get at the rum and aqua vitae – is impossible. As he writes, the narrator sometimes thinks himself into the middle of the scene, allowing indications of his presence to show in the first-person pronouns of stanzas 34, 42 and 95 (cancelling them, on second thought, in stanza 28). Seen from this perspective, the wreck of the ironically named *Trinidada* ('Holy Trinity') is unequivocally terrible. But Byron is also the conscious inventor of a fiction, aware when he archly says of the one brittle oar in the long-boat, 'I wish they had had a pair' (II.70), that such a gift was entirely in his giving. In this detached, manipulative role he feels free to isolate and examine the absurdities of human behaviour under stress, all the time keeping what he jokingly stigmatized as the 'atrocious reader' (XIV.97) off-balance by the unpredictability of his oscillations between sympathy and satire.

Juan's tutor, the scholar and cleric Pedrillo, for instance, begins as a comic butt. As soon as the ship is in danger, the roles of master and pupil are reversed. Juan, guarding the door of the spirit-room from those members of the crew who 'thought it would be becoming to die drunk' (II.35), finds himself also fending off Pedrillo, who 'was for some rum a disappointed suitor' (36). Pious lamentations and vows of irrevocable reformation follow, in the midst of which the self-obsessed Pedrillo swears at a poor Christian who asks him for absolution. It is Juan, 'as if they had exchanged their care' (56), who manages to secure his weeping tutor a place in the longboat (Byron may have been remembering Polidori, the unfortunate personal physician he engaged to accompany him on his travels in 1816, and then had to nurse through a suc-cession of illnesses). And it is Juan again who looks after and even shares the meagre forepaw of his spaniel with a man much older than himself, now immobilized with fear. Yet, surprisingly, when the lottery dictates that Pedrillo is to be the first human killed and eaten, he accepts his ghastly fate with dignity and a religious composure in sharp contrast to his earlier, absurd attempts to bargain with his Creator. The narrator treats this death respectfully – and then moves on immediately to the grotesque matter of the surgeon's 'fee', earned in this case for bleeding a patient to death: a 'first choice of morsels for his pains' (77). When last mentioned, in connection with the madness which overcame those who committed 'a species of self-slaughter, / In washing down Pedrillo with salt water' (102), the confusion of a Christian name with something that sounds like an hors-d'œuvre is both horrible and funny.

There is something about the way Byron handles Pedrillo that is reminiscent of Shakespeare's Holofernes or Jaques, apparently irredeemable objects of mockery who suddenly command respect. Although he liked to poke fun at the 'Bardolatry' of his contemporaries and even, mischievously, to denigrate Shakespeare, Byron's detailed knowledge of the plays, both major and minor, was matched in the period only by that of Coleridge. He could afford, in Italy, to shock Leigh Hunt by pointing out that he did not own a copy of Shakespeare because of the massive amount already stored in his memory, most of it (as *Don Juan* continually demonstrates) on hair-trigger, associative recall. The poem is seamed, to an extent rivalled only by its use of the Old Testament, with Shakespearean quotation and allusion. The Bible, though it continued to haunt Byron's vestigially Calvinist conscience, tended now to activate his resistance to revealed religion. Shakespeare's generosity towards his characters, that reluctance to pass final judgements on them which Keats described as 'negative capability', was on the other hand something Byron found increasingly sympathetic. Certainly it is related to the way he looks at individuals in his own poem.

Often, as in Canto IX, which is coloured throughout by *Hamlet* in ways that go far beyond specific quotation from that play, Byron will allow his memory of a particular Shakespearean episode or situation to shape and complicate what he is writing. Behind the shipwreck in Canto II lie not only the nautical disasters documented by Dalyell, Bligh and 'Foulweather Jack', but also the opening scene of *The Tempest* with its mixture of terror and comedy, its inversion of social hierarchies in the face of death, its precise and detailed seamanship, and fantastic, dreamlike issue. A seasoned traveller in these parts, and also a stickler for facts, Byron knew perfectly well that a man cast away in the vicinity of the Gulf of Lyons could not possibly be washed up on one of the islands of the Cyclades, some two thousand kilometres distant in the Aegean. Juan's arrival there is no more subject to realistic interrogation than the voyage of Prospero and the infant Miranda from Milan (which has, in fact, no port) in a 'rotten carcase of a butt', without tackling, sail or mast, to an island which may lie somewhere in the Mediterranean between Naples and Tunis, or may with equal persuasiveness be located in the New World. Significantly, Byron's Juan awakes on this Greek island to find it controlled by a strong and difficult father possessed of a beautiful daughter, his sole child. There, the story of Ferdinand, Miranda and Prospero will be played out again, but with a tragic conclusion.

'Passion's child'

Haidée (the name, which Byron accented only after Canto II, means 'a caress') is dangerous. Wave-worn and starving, Juan recovers consciousness on the beach where the sea has flung him to find that her 'small mouth / Seem'd almost prying into his for breath' (II. 113). The glance darted from eyes 'black as death' disconcertingly calls to mind 'the snake late coil'd, who pours his length, / And hurls at once his venom and his strength' (II. 117). Haidée, as becomes apparent at the end of her story, is 'a lioness' (IV. 44), very much her father's child. Yet she is also Juan's (and, in a sense, the narrator's) one perfect and unmatchable love: an ideal miraculously found, lost, and never to be recovered. Unlike Julia, obliterated in the poem after stanza 208 of Canto II ('But Juan! had he quite forgotten Julia? / And should he have forgotten her so soon?'), Haidée will still be remembered, by the narrator at least, as late as Canto XV and in a context (the house party at Norman Abbey) as different as possible from her own.

That strain of Moorish blood which Julia inherited from

her great great grandmother, Haidée possesses in a far more immediate and concentrated form: 'her mother was a Moorish maid, from Fez' (IV.54). Her father, moreover, is a Greek pirate and slave-trader, not a Spanish nobleman, and she has grown up further south than Julia, with all that this implies for the narrator about the incendiary effects of 'that indecent sun' (I.63). Certainly Haidée, 'Passion's child', becomes 'Nature's bride' (II.202) in a radically different sense from the one Wordsworth imagines for Lucy in his poem 'Three years she grew in sun and shower'. Nature treats Lucy as a favourite, bestowing on her qualities and graces, vaguely feminine but unmistakably chaste, borrowed from the mountains, streams and trees of the 'happy dell' in which she lives, together with an ability to share the inner life of such things that had once been Wordsworth's own. Haidée's island paradise is equally unspoiled and beautiful, but Byron insists that the Aegean, even though in its quiet moods 'the small ripple spilt upon the beach / Scarcely o'erpass'd the cream of your champagne' (II.178), remains the same appalling ocean about which Juan already knows too much. When, restored to health, he wanders forth at twilight hand in hand with Haidée 'over the shining pebbles and the shells' (II.184), the two are simultaneously aware both of how lovely it all is, and how vast, alien and impersonal:

> The silent ocean, and the starlight bay,
>   The twilight glow, which momently grew less,
> The voiceless sands, and dropping caves, that lay
>   Around them, made them to each other press.
>
> (II.188)

Those sea caves, in one of which they finally rest, 'worn and wild receptacles / Work'd by the storms, yet work'd as it were plann'd' (II.184), prompt no Wordsworthian empathy. Random products of the wind and waves, they only *seem* 'plann'd'. The splendours of Nature confirm for Haidée and Juan the separateness of their own existence, impelling them towards each other, and towards the 'natural' (II.194) – in Byron's sense of the word – consummation of their love.

Although the island on which Haidée dwells is not unin-
habited — her father, Lambro, maintains a large band of
servants and domestics — it is oddly isolated and special. The
beauty of Haidée, 'the greatest heiress of the Eastern Isles'
(II.128), has been rumoured outside it, and she has already
rejected several suitors. Yet, like Shakespeare's Miranda, she
is entirely spontaneous and innocent, flying 'to her young mate
like a young bird' (II.190), neither offering nor exacting vows
of constancy or marriage. Unlike Prospero, Lambro has not
seen fit to teach his daughter how to read and write. She is
illiterate (II.162) even in her own tongue, and altogether
ignorant of Juan's. The narrator, relating Juan's later amorous
escapades in Turkey, Russia and England, will quietly pass
over the question of the language barrier. With Haidée, on
the other hand, he stresses it. She and Juan are obliged to
communicate initially 'by dint of fingers and of eyes' (II.163)
and, although he does gradually learn a few words and phrases
of Romaic, their spoken language, 'like to that of birds, /
Known but to them' (IV.14), never begins to approximate
what they think and then can express and understand through
their senses: by way of gestures, looks, physical contact,
including love-making, and other non-verbal means.

It is the paradox of this love that, although so dependent
upon the body, it is at the same time spiritual and transcendent.
Juan and Haidée become 'one flesh' in a manner that re-vitalizes
that old cliché. Living only for and in each other, their perfect
physical relationship incorporates a harmony of souls. Such a
love, Byron insists, although occasionally claimed by others,
is almost invariably 'a factitious state, / An opium dream of
too much youth and reading' (IV.19). Here, it is lived out for
a time by a sixteen-year-old boy and a girl of seventeen, neither
of whom has ever opened a romantic novel. The narrator does
not pretend to be part of their story, as he had briefly done
with earlier events of the poem and was to do again at Norman
Abbey. Yet his presence as commentator, as opposed to the
dispassionate teller of a tale, increases enormously as this story
unfolds. From stanza 154 of Canto II, where Juan first sits
down to breakfast with Haidée, through that moment at the

mid-point of Canto IV in which she dies, digressions, flagrantly calling attention to themselves (and of a length anticipated only by stanzas 122–34 of Canto I), become an unignorable feature of the poem.

Apart from the introductory and concluding stanzas, in the early sections of *Don Juan* the narrator had kept his eye far more fixedly on the tale he was telling than had been the case in *Beppo*. An omnipresent personality, he punctuated them continually with asides but never, as in his first experiment with *ottava rima*, allowed digression to tyrannize over story. The single, conspicuous exception ('We'll talk of that anon. – 'Tis sweet to hear / At midnight ...') had an obvious purpose: to make the reader experience (as opposed merely to being informed of) a lapse of time separating June, when Juan and Julia first make love, and November, when the narrator chooses to let their relationship be discovered. The digressions which mark the Haidée episode are different from this, both in function and character.

'But to resume' (II. 157), 'Return we to Don Juan' (II. 167), 'The coast – I think it was the coast that I / Was just describing – Yes, it *was* the coast' (II. 181), 'But to return' (II. 211), 'Meantime Apollo plucks me by the ear, / And tells me to resume my story here' (IV. 7); Byron even signals the end of one of these excursions ('But let me to my story: I must own, / If I have any fault, it is digression', III. 96), and then proceeds not only to digress for five stanzas more, but after returning to the narrative ('T'our tale', 101) for barely one, immediately hares off again ('Ave Maria! o'er the earth and sea', 101) for eighty-two lines (interrupted by 'But I'm digressing' at 110) until he is brought up short by the end of the canto. The psychology behind these outrageous delaying tactics is clear. Through them the narrator registers his profound reluctance, when it comes to the point, to bring Haidée's story to its inevitable tragic end. That is why it takes him no fewer than one thousand one hundred and seven lines to let her father, Lambro, the agent of the catastrophe, take the few steps required from the island's harbour where he has just disembarked to the hall in his house where he will surprise Haidée asleep in her lover's arms, will sell Juan into slavery, and so cause the death of his own dearly-loved daughter and her unborn child.

The digressions themselves, however, reveal far more about the Juan/Haidée relationship than simply the narrator's emotional disinclination to destroy it. Initially, they serve to remind the reader of what love – and, more particularly, marriage ('A sad, sour, sober beverage', III. 5) – is like for ordinary people, of how quickly men and women who once thought their passion inexhaustible begin to tire of and judge each other: 'Think you, if Laura had been Petrarch's wife, / He would have written sonnets all his life?' (III. 8). Reflections of this kind reinforce the extraordinary and quite special nature of Juan and Haidée's love, from a position well outside it. Then, towards the end, they alter their character, hammering upon the idea that in the case of Juan and Haidée, death is, in fact, the best gift the gods could bestow. That such paradisal happiness could be realized even briefly is a species of miracle. It cannot possibly be sustained. Even on the island, time and ageing are bound, slowly and ignominiously, to enforce a division that Lambro, at least, accomplishes at a single stroke.

Byron insists that the love of Juan and Haidée is mythic, like that of the immortals. 'Their faces were not made for wrinkles, their / Pure blood to stagnate, their great hearts to fail' (IV. 9), nor were they intended 'in the real world to fill / A busy character in the dull scene' (IV. 15). Yet, even during the few months that their idyll lasts, there are ominous signs of a decline from the purity of those first, half-naked embraces beside the Aegean. Haidée, falsely informed of her father's death at sea, and too much obsessed with Juan to mourn in any but a perfunctory fashion, seizes upon the opportunity to install her clandestine lover, at last, in her father's house. There the two of them, surrounded by black eunuchs, dancing girls, dwarfs and a turncoat poet modelled on Robert Southey, preside over an apparently endless revel, 'which turn'd the isle into a place of pleasure' (III. 39). Patroness now of 'gazelles and cats', of people who 'gain / Their bread as ministers and favourites – (that's / To say, by degradation)' (III. 68), amid a clutter of opulent but unnecessary things, Haidée herself, although ' 'tis very silly / "To gild refined gold, or paint the lily" ' (III. 76), even takes to using cosmetics to heighten a beauty in no need of such artificial assistance. There is no diminution as yet in the quality of her and Juan's ecstatic love. It is impossible, however, not to feel it menaced by the way of life they have now adopted, and by those stern sentences from the Persian moralists which glare down on them from the wall-hangings, like 'The words which shook Belshazzar in his hall, / And took his kingdom from him' (III. 65), but which they do not heed. Into this complicated ambience Byron introduces Lambro: 'the mildest-manner'd man / That ever scuttled ship, or cut a throat' (III. 41), and refuses to treat him simply as a villain.

An ordinary fisherman in his youth, Lambro has for some years operated, 'like Peter the Apostle' (II. 126), as a fisher of men, although scarcely to the same end. He lies in wait for merchant vessels, confiscates their cargoes and sells their passengers and crew into slavery. These methods of raising cash, the narrator slyly insists, are equivalent to those which in a prime minister are called 'taxation', though Lambro him-self is content to claim a humbler role, and merely practises as 'a sea-attorney' (III. 14). Passengers too old or infirm to be saleable he throws overboard − a literalization of their usual fate in 'polite' society. As for his lucrative participation in the slave trade, Greece under Turkish rule is herself 'a land of slaves' (III. Song 16), as Haidée's visiting poet points out. Stingingly aware of that fact, Lambro has turned 'from a slave to an enslaver' (III. 53), waging war upon all nations 'in vengeance of [his country's] degradation' (III. 55). He is ruthless and cruel, but at the same time so admirably self-controlled, so refined and moderate in his tastes and personal habits, as to represent (the narrator affirms) 'a loss to good society' (III. 41). His daughter, Haidée, is the only creature on earth he loves, his sole human tie, and he does not take kindly to the discovery that his home has been taken over, and himself summarily replaced in her affections, by a stranger.

Juan, who had found it relatively easy to overwhelm Julia's

husband Alphonso in a scuffle, stands no chance against this man. When Byron finally allows Lambro to confront the un-suspecting pair, it is Haidée who prevents Juan from being killed, interposing herself between him and her father's cocked pistol, 'as one who champion'd human fears' (IV. 43). She and Lambro are two of a kind. As a result, Juan is merely taken prisoner by the old man's attendants, bound, and shipped away to be sold in the slave market at Constantinople. Haidée herself collapses without ever knowing what happened to him: 'A vein had burst, and her sweet lips' pure dyes / Were dabbled with the deep blood which ran o'er' (IV. 59). She falls into a coma, awaking from it with her reason shattered, and then sinks, after twelve days and nights, into death. The narrator observes the progressive stages of her dissolution rather as Byron himself had observed the last minutes of the criminal whose execution he witnessed at Rome in 1817: with an opera-glass in hand to pick up every detail because 'one should see everything once – with attention' (BLJ V. 230), but psycho-logically distressed to the point of scarcely being able to hold it steady. It is a mysteriously all-embracing catastrophe. The island itself becomes 'desolate and bare, / Its dwellings down, its tenants past away' (IV. 72), overtaken by a fate even more bleak than that of the castle in Keats' 'Eve of St Agnes' after the lovers flee away into the storm. The story of Haidée and Lambro is still known and told or sung on other islands, but where they actually lived, for reasons on which the narrator refuses to elaborate, even their graves are lost.

'You've heard of Raucocanti?'

A paradisal vision disappears with Haidée, never to return in the poem, except fleetingly in Canto VIII, as Byron wistfully contemplates the primitive but free life of the American frontiersman Daniel Boone in the backwoods of Kentucky – itself, significantly, a legend of the past – or in the parody offered by London suburbia, with its ' "Rows" most modestly called "Paradise", / Which Eve might quit without much sacrifice' (XI. 21). Whenever Byron specifically remembers the biblical Garden of Eden in Cantos II—IV he is haunted by an underlying consciousness of transgression and sin, something disturbingly at odds with his otherwise celebratory attitude towards the lovers. The observation that 'they were happy, — happy in the illicit / Indulgence of their innocent desires' (III.13), for instance, where 'innocent' confronts 'illicit' as an unresolved contradiction, seems provoked by allusions to Dante and to Milton's *Paradise Lost* three stanzas before. Old Testament Eden, however, is not the only paradigm shattered in this section of the poem. Byron himself, as G. Wilson Knight once observed, was perpetually trying (and failing) to live his own life with the necessary intensity, the total commitment of great art, to discover in daily existence the qualities of myth. This is something that Juan and Haidée, for a time, accomplish. The ultimate destruction of their relationship is all the more poignant because it violates expectations carried over quite deliberately into the poem from Homeric and Shakespearean romance.

Byron relies in the Haidée section upon the *Odyssey*, in particular the Nausicaä episode in Book IV, and (in Lambro's homecoming) upon Odysseus' return to a riotous house which no longer recognizes him as its master. In both cases, what in Homer had turned out happily in Byron leads to disaster. 'An honest gentleman at his return', as the narrator observes, 'may not have the good fortune of Ulysses' (III.23). He is likely to find his Penelope unchaste, 'and that his Argus bites him by — the breeches' (*ibid.*). This, effectively, is what happens to Lambro. Even so, Haidée finds, unlike Nausicaä, that introducing her father to the handsome castaway she has rescued is the way to wreck the stranger's fortunes, not to mend them. Parallels with *The Tempest* turn out to be equally disconcerting.

Shakespeare's play was explicitly in Byron's mind at stanza 134 of Canto II. Just after Haidée tears herself reluctantly away from the sleeping stranger, he toyed with a final couplet about dreams which leave 'No "baseless fabric"', but '"a wreck behind"', a phrase adapted from Prospero's famous valediction: 'Our revels now are ended.' He cancelled the line in the end, but the shadowy presence throughout these cantos of that other island trio of irascible father, shipwrecked lover and disobedient daughter remains, helping to define what might have been against what, in Byron's more pessimistic handling of the paradigm, actually is. Even more bitter and disabused than Prospero, Lambro's affections are similarly bound up with this one child who shares his essentially solitary existence. But the anger which Prospero had merely feigned against Ferdinand, 'lest too light winning / Make the prize light', the contempt for his 'silly' sword and threat of fetters and forced labour, are no longer steps towards a happy ending. Shakespeare's story re-told goes wrong before the reader's eyes, as life rebels against the optimistic patterning of art.

When it is all over, with Haidée, Lambro and the place where they lived swept away, a crisis declares itself in *Don Juan*. The shipwreck and the island romance into which it led had comprised a clearly defined second unit of the poem. The problem, however, of what could possibly succeed this unit was far more acute than the question of what to do with Juan after the mingled mockery and tears of the Julia affair. The episode of the island, although by no means lacking in humour along the way, comes to an unequivocally tragic conclusion, ending in a desolation which leaves neither the narrator nor the reader with anything at which to laugh. The only major event (including the shipwreck and the siege of Ismail) of which this is true, it threatens not only the balance, the characteristically mixed tone, of *Don Juan*, but the very possibility of its continuation. Byron recognized this. If Juan was to overleap this catastrophe while retaining the reader's interest and respect, some way had to be found of letting go of Haidée and the experience she epitomized without forgetting, let alone dishonouring, either.

Byron's characteristically brilliant solution to the problem is to be found in stanzas 80–94 of Canto IV. When Juan stumbles up, wounded and fettered, still weak from loss of blood, onto the deck of that slave-ship in which he has been quite literally 'cabin'd, cribb'd, confin'd' (IV. 75) since his violent expulsion from the island, he discovers that although he appears to have been transported from the world of Shakespearean romance to that of tragedy, at least the players are there with him in Elsinore. They are players of a very special and composite kind. Raucocanti and his associates testify to the deep impression made upon Byron by Shakespeare's use of the travelling actors in *Hamlet*, the tragedians of the city, but also to his memories of service on the Drury Lane Committee in London. More immediately, they derive from his residence in Venice and regular attendance at the Fenice there: an opera-house which, as he rapturously assured his sister Augusta (BLJ V. 160), was not only cheaper but much finer than anything London could provide. Raucocanti, the loquacious buffo of that modest Italian opera company, all of whose members have been sold into slavery by its 'Machiavelian impresario' (IV. 82), is both Shakespearean and Venetian: yet another example of the kind of artistic cross-breeding encouraged by Byron's Italian exile.

Raucocanti's function in *Don Juan* is crucial. For one thing, the little buffo allows Byron to build a bridge between *The Tempest* and *Hamlet*. *Hamlet* is a work of great overall importance in the poem, not only because of the sheer number of verbal echoes, but because its preoccupations are also those of long stretches of *Don Juan*. Unlike the other Romantics, Byron was drawn equally to the melancholy, introspective figure of the prince himself and to other characters and aspects of the work: Polonius, Gertrude, the grave-digger, the ghost or, as here in Canto IV, the travelling actors. He was also keenly alive, as Coleridge and Goethe for instance were not, to the comic dimension of the play. This may be one reason why he found it so easy to sense the underlying connection between *Hamlet* and *The Tempest* – the noblest of Shakespeare's revenge plays, as it has been called – and so to remember Elsinore, as well as Prospero's island, in a Mediterranean context.

There are flickers of *Hamlet* back in Canto III, in Lambro's reaction to the unbuttoned festivities in his garden ('to one deem'd dead returning, / This revel seem'd a curious mode of mourning', 49), nudging as it does at the reader's memory of the 'mirth in funeral' and 'dirge in marriage' accompanying Claudius and Gertrude's over-hasty wedding. An obscurely troubled but resilient Haidée is said before the catastrophe to be 'defying augury' (IV. 24), like Hamlet before the fencing match. It is, however, with Raucocanti that Byron's creative use of Shakespeare is most striking. Just as, in Shakespeare's play, the actors arrive to cheer everybody up — including, for the moment, young Hamlet — after the death of the old king and his widow's indecorous re-marriage, so Byron is able to use their equivalents in *Don Juan* to persuade the reader that nothing is ever quite the end, that even after the painful, protracted and seemingly conclusive disaster of the island, the show can and will go on.

Raucocanti's dramatic monologue (IV. 82–9), the quite unsolicited, scabrous and detailed personal account he offers Juan of the other members of the travelling company, is as brilliant as anything Browning ever produced in the genre. Like Browning's 'A Toccata of Galuppi's' (1855), Raucocanti's monologue draws inspiration from the festive, the carnivalesque, in Italian life. But it shocks at the same time that it delights. As Raucocanti compulsively gabbles on, exposing in the process the failings of his own character quite as much as those of other members of the troupe, the reader suddenly remembers the extent to which Juan and Haidée's relationship had been independent of the spoken word. Not until she was obliged to plead with Lambro for Juan's life did Haidée become eloquent. Only six words of Juan's (again addressed to Lambro) are recorded during his entire stay on the island: 'Not while this arm is free' (IV. 40), as he brandishes his futile sabre. The very introduction of these speeches signals the end of the idyll. But that idyll only really becomes a thing of the past, allowing Byron's poem to continue, when Raucocanti embarks on his monologue and, in doing so, forcibly reminds both Juan and the reader that all the time there has been a world elsewhere.

It is an intensely social world. Raucocanti's little company, tenor and bass, prima donna, baritone, castrato and dancers, suddenly presents Juan with a microcosm of the contemporary European civilization he had for a time escaped. As the buffo continues describing the idiosyncrasies of his fellow performers and how they live, the images of Haidée's island — sea-cave and sunsets, throngs of dancers, story-tellers, the snow-white ram, its horns wreathed with flowers by childish hands, even that dubious itinerant, the poet who sang 'The Isles of Greece' — recede. They come to seem like the stuff that dreams are made on, acquiring the quality of an operatic scene: entrancing but unreal, something constructed out of canvas and false lights, peopled by players who, once the show is over, will be at one another's throats, intriguing to carry off 'Count Cesare Cicogna / From an old Roman princess at Bologna' (IV. 83), or scheming to get their relatives a job.

Raucocanti's world is of an indubitably fallen kind, but it is remarkably difficult to dismiss or even condemn. He himself may be a 'busy character', but the scene in which he plays is not, after all, 'dull' (IV. 15) when Byron comes once again to confront it. On one level a blackguard, as the narrator admits, certainly malicious and spiteful, Raucocanti nonetheless bears himself under trying circumstances 'with some gaiety and grace' (IV. 81). Byron may again be thinking of *The Tempest* when he makes the little buffo cheerfully press Juan to come and hear him sing next year 'at the fair of Lugo' (IV. 88). He has, after all, no more assurance of ever being released from slavery than Shakespeare's Stephano has of being able to get off the island and exhibit Caliban in England for cash. There is something endearing about the man's irrepressible optimism and self-regard ('You've heard of Raucocanti? — I'm the man', IV. 88), about the aplomb with which he accepts what has happened to him and immediately sets about speculating how, if only 'the Sultan has a taste for song' (IV. 82), the whole seedy troupe may yet be in a way to prosper.

Things quite as improbable had been known to happen, as Byron's own note on the passage points out. Of the fictional hijacking of the Italian opera company, he wrote:

This is a fact. A few years ago a man engaged a company for some foreign theatre; embarked them at an Italian port, and carrying them to Algiers, sold them all. One of the women, returned from her captivity, I heard sing, by a strange coincidence, in Rossini's opera of 'L'Italiana in Algeri', at Venice, in the beginning of 1817.

Byron was delighted by the 'strange coincidence' that allowed him to hear a woman who had escaped from slavery in Algiers singing in an opera whose plot is about the escape of an Italian girl from the harem of the bey of Algiers. It confirmed him in his cherished belief that there was something wrong about things '*all fiction*', that there should always be 'some foundation of fact for the most airy fabric', pure invention being 'but the talent of a liar' (BLJ V.203). A vertiginous compound of imagination and truth, in a way validating the fantastic plot of Rossini's opera, his recollection of the strange fortunes of the Italian singer at the Fenice also helped Byron to set his epic on an even keel again, after an episode which had carried an abnormally light ballast of fact. It even seems to have suggested where the poem could go next: to a harem, although Juan will meet Dudù and Gulbeyaz in Constantinople, not Algiers.

The reader is never told what became of Raucocanti himself, left chained to the tenor, a man he hated with what Byron, remembering his days at Drury Lane, identifies (in a double sense) as 'a hate found only on the stage' (IV.93). Although the narrator promises, at the end of the canto, to describe the various destinies of the captives 'in further song' (117), he never does so. Only Juan himself is carried over into the next canto. Raucocanti and his associates vanish into that slipstream of oblivion that has already claimed other characters in the poem. In ensuing cantos, it will also swallow up the woman Byron is about to introduce as his 'third heroine' (VI.7): Gulbeyaz, the fiery sultana who dominates Cantos V and VI, as well as her rival Dudù. In the case of Raucocanti and the opera troupe, Byron's reticence does not matter. Like the players in *Hamlet*, who also disappear after Act III into a future about which nothing is known, they have fulfilled their purpose in the poem.

'Our hero and third heroine'

On the island, the narrator had counterpoised the single-minded ecstasies of Juan and Haidée with sobering reminders of what love and marriage tend to be like in that ordinary, social world

which he and his readers share. There, 'domestic doings' –
Byron was defiantly remembering his original epigraph,
Domestica facta – constitute 'true love's antithesis' (III.8).
Men, especially married men, 'grow ashamed of being so very
fond' (III.7). They hanker after variety and change, as the
narrator himself has recently been guilty of doing at a Venetian
masquerade (II.209–11), while women, their first passion over,
come to adore the condition of being in love more than any of
its individual objects. Haidée's early death at least spares her
such sordid recognitions. Juan, on the other hand, is doubly
sold into slavery. Although released from his actual fetters in
Constantinople, he will remain the thrall of imperfection, and
of time.

It is true that Haidée – whose fate he never learns – fades
from his memory less rapidly than did Julia. Loyally unmoved
by the physical charms of the Italian girl to whom for a while
he is chained, Juan subsequently weeps when the anonymous
Englishman exhibited beside him in the slave-market inquires
into the cause of his present misfortune. This admirably cool,
unruffled stranger, although introduced early in Canto V, is
not given a personal name until Canto VII, two hundred and
twenty nine stanzas after his first appearance, when a direct
question from Catherine's General Suwarrow suddenly elicits
it. Up to this point the narrator refers to him, however incon-
veniently, merely as 'the other', or as Juan's 'acquaintance',
'companion' or 'friend'. A mercenary soldier with the Russian
army, captured at the siege of Widdin, the older man is
sympathetic about Juan's lost love, but from the vantage-point
of one for whom such emotions are a thing of the past:
' "I cried upon my first wife's dying day, / And also when my
second ran away: / My third – " – "Your third!", quoth
Juan, turning round' (V.19–20). Juan's astonishment only
hastens the revelation that his interlocutor, not content with
committing bigamy, has run away from *her*.

When finally disclosed in Canto VII, the stranger's name
turns out to be 'John Johnson', the English version, in a
doubled form, of Juan's own. It is probably true that Byron
was remembering 'Gentleman' John Jackson, the celebrated

pugilist who had acted as his athletic coach during the London years. More importantly, Johnson is a prefiguration of Juan himself at thirty, an age which Byron's plan for the poem apparently was not going to allow him to reach: his impetuosity and youthful illusions gone, humorous, stoical and (like his seventeenth-century Spanish original) a cynic about women, including Fortune, that 'female moderately fickle' (V.7). Thirty, however, was also Byron's own age when he began *Don Juan*, as the narrator confesses in Canto I ('But now at thirty years my hair is gray', 213), before going on to lament the loss of his youth and (erroneously, as it turned out) his former capacity to fall passionately in love. For a time, Juan enters into dialogue with a shadowy future self who also looks and sounds remarkably like the narrator: a narrator who briefly invades the poem here in order to confront his hero with attitudes and opinions hitherto reserved for the reader alone:

> Love's the first net which spreads its deadly mesh;
>   Ambition, Avarice, Vengeance, Glory, glue
> The glittering lime-twigs of our latter days,
>   Where still we flutter on for pence or praise.
>
> (V.22)

Although it is Johnson, as he is later identified, who tells Juan this, the voice is Byron's own.

Byron's physical courage, his coolness and practical good sense under potentially lethal circumstances, whether storms at sea, a murder in the street, or a revolution, were never questioned even by his enemies. This side of himself he projected onto Juan's companion, a man who stands in the slave-market nursing a wounded arm while awaiting a buyer, 'with such *sang-froid* that greater / Could scarce be shown even by a mere spectator' (V.11). (Significantly, Byron later chose to insert his digression about the death of the military commandant of Ravenna, and his own futile attempt to save him, immediately after the introduction of this fictional character.) When Juan subsequently suggests hitting their purchaser, the black eunuch Baba, over the head and making a dash for freedom, his new friend sees at once that as they have no idea how they got into the mysterious walled enclosure through which they are being led, so they would not have the faintest notion how to get out. Besides, they could do with some dinner. Even their guide's suggestion that conversion to the Muslim faith, accompanied by circumcision, would improve their condition, a proposal which enrages Juan, the older man tactfully promises to consider – after he has dined.

Although the narrator is never explicit on this point, Baba has presumably bargained for both slaves, not for Juan alone, in order to protect his mistress, the sultana, from suspicion at having singled out so egregiously handsome a young stranger for private purchase. Whatever the rationale on the level of pure story, the cool Horatian indifference of Juan's companion, his adaptability to strange and alarming circumstances, coupled with an uncompromising masculinity, throw into relief not only the *naiveté* and emotionalism of the young Spaniard, but the considerable feminine component in his nature. Juan may be outraged when Baba orders him to put on the attire of a harem girl, consenting only when threatened with the sinister attentions of 'Those who will leave you of no sex at all' (V. 75). He has to be cautioned about the manly length of his stride as they advance towards the women's quarters. Yet, even as Gulbeyaz had earlier picked him out from among a throng of other men in the slave-market, so the sultan's masculine eye will be drawn at once to 'Juanna' among a throng of other (and deeply envious) concubines: ' "I see you've bought another girl; 'tis pity / That a mere christian should be half so pretty" ' (V. 155). Byron was almost certainly remembering here Count Almaviva's approving notice of the page Cherubino, strategically disguised as a maid attending on the countess, in Mozart's *The Marriage of Figaro* – a boy's part actually scored for a mezzo-soprano.

When introducing Haidée and her maid Zoe, the narrator had announced that he would tell the reader all about them at once, because 'I hate all mystery, and that air / Of clap-trap, which your recent poets prize' (II. 124). The Julia episode was handled, for the most part, in a similarly straightforward fashion. With his 'third heroine' (VI. 7) Gulbeyaz, however, and the events she sets in motion, the narrator becomes singularly devious and indirect, no longer privileging the reader. He or she initially knows no more than Juan himself why Baba has chosen to buy him, to what place he is then transported, or why he should be separated so quickly from his companion and obliged to adopt female dress. As the hero moves 'room by room / Through glittering galleries, and o'er marble floors' (V. 85), the Ottoman profusion of sofas and silken carpets, in-door fountains, gems and gold inevitably recalls the splendours of that earlier indoor setting, Lambro's house (the decorative style of which had been Turkish, not Greek), except that this establishment is on a far larger and more lavish, indeed un-mistakably royal, scale. There had been eunuchs and dwarfs in Lambro's house too, but the former (unlike Baba) were unim-portant, and the latter did not appall, unlike those 'misshapen pigmies, deaf and dumb' (V. 88) who guard the bronze portals of the harem – when they are not engaged in strangling, according to custom, one of the innumerable male aspirants to a father's throne. At the centre of it all, as on the island, Juan and the reader find a lady, but she is not (apart from her beauty) much like Haidée.

Only after Juan has been left alone with Gulbeyaz does the narrator reveal that he has been purchased to 'Serve a sultana's sensual phantasy' (V. 126). Imperious and spoiled, Gulbeyaz is not herself responsible for Juan's ignominious disguise. She has merely ordered him to be acquired, leaving Baba to contrive the means of smuggling him into the harem. The most recent and therefore favourite of the sultan's four wives (he also possesses roughly one thousand concubines), Gulbeyaz has twenty-six years to Juan's sixteen: three more than Julia, and nine more than Haidée. She too, in a sense, is innocent, but it is not, as theirs had been, the innocence of inexperience. She has simply been so accustomed all her life to the immediate gratification of her slightest whim, and to regarding other people (with one exception) as her slaves, as never to have considered anyone else's wishes or feelings, let alone the possibility of her own being denied.

Juan's ludicrous situation and, in particular, his female

attire, undercut the dignity of his refusal to 'pair' with the sultana on command. She is shocked and bewildered by the tears that spring to his eyes as he remembers Haidée. On the other hand, when the tumult of her own emotions resolves into tears as well, the effect on Juan is electric. A haughty and infuriated woman he could withstand, but not one who weeps. He is rapidly reconsidering his position when the arrival of the sultan, who has decided to honour Gulbeyaz with a marital visit, puts an end not only to this episode but, for a time, to Byron's entire poem as well. Here, at the conclusion of Canto V, he stopped writing *Don Juan* for over a year. It was not the first break in its composition, but it was the longest and also the most consequential.

Although he put a brave and defiant face on it, Byron had been shaken by the savage reviews, coupled with the disapproval of his friends, which greeted Cantos I and II. He himself worried that the originally enormous Canto III, which he decided to divide into two in February 1820, was spiritless and dull, while being as likely as its predecessors to scandalize the reading public. It might, he feared, even cost him the guardianship of his two children. Certainly, neither Murray nor Byron's other friends in England were eager to see III and IV through the press. Much occupied at the time with the Italian Carbonari movement, with Teresa Guiccioli's separation from her husband, and with *Marino Faliero*, the first of his political plays, Byron did not embark on Canto V until October of that year. He finished it the following month, arranged for its anonymous publication together with III and IV, but refused to correct proofs for V. On 6 July 1821 he informed Murray that he was proceeding no further with *Don Juan*, claiming that the Countess Guiccioli, who had read the poem in French translation, had made him promise to abandon it.

There was probably some truth in this allegation – certainly Teresa detested *Don Juan* – but it was by no means the whole explanation. The Italian epigraph, from Berni's recast *Orlando Innamorato*, which Murray was instructed but failed to append to Cantos III and IV ('Di Sopra vi contai questa novella / Quando ... / Credo che fu de l'altro libro al fine' – 'I told you this story earlier / When ... / I think that was at the end of another book') seems to betray on Byron's part (however unwarrantable it may seem to the reader) a certain self-mocking sense of repetition and sameness in his conduct of the poem: the loss of Julia reiterated in the loss of Haidée, Juan a reluctant sea-voyager for the second time, bound for yet another amorous escapade which will render him, once again, the rival of a man much older than himself. Increasingly involved with plans for an Italian revolution, he may well have become impatient with *Don Juan*, and in particular with its characteristic blend, in Cantos I–IV, of satire and romance. What political teeth the poem so far manifested (as in the stanzas attacking Wellington, or the Dedication), he had been obliged in large part to remove at the insistence of his publisher and friends. The story, moreover, in Constantinople, was impinging upon territory already wearisomely familiar, as far as he was concerned, from the early cantos of *Childe Harold* and his eastern tales.

In a letter of 12 May 1821 Byron observed that 'I have been latterly employed a good deal more on politics than on anything else' (BLJ VIII. 115). The Italian uprising had, by that date, failed. Political concerns, however, continued to occupy Byron's attention in *Sardanapalus* and *The Two Foscari*, the plays that followed *Marino Faliero*, and in the third of his *ottava rima* masterpieces, *The Vision of Judgement*, written in September 1821 as a response to Southey's absurd apotheosis of George III. At the same time he renewed his long-standing (and, for contemporaries, quite shocking) quarrel with the God of the Old Testament in the verse dramas *Cain* and *Heaven and Earth*. *Don Juan*, when he at last returned to it, in secret, some time in January 1822, had, inevitably, to change direction: to reflect, if it was to continue at all, both Byron's intervening commitments and interests, and a new, more serious purpose for the poem. That, given the farcical situation set up at the end of Canto V, with a transvestite Juan about to spend his first night in a harem and Gulbeyaz obliged to feign sexual transport in the arms of an elderly, abhorred, but royal spouse, was by no means easy.

'A brain-spattering, windpipe-slitting art'

By 14 April 1822, when Byron at last disclosed to a visitor his
resumption of *Don Juan*, he had in fact been engaged with
Canto VI, on and off, for some months. Work on this canto
and its successor proceeded slowly, as McGann has established,
although Byron later did his best, by almost completely
obliterating the dates of composition on the manuscript, to
obscure this fact. It was July before he broke the news to his
publisher, by which time he had finally hit his stride. External
circumstances − the death of his daughter Allegra, followed
by that of Shelley, his own ill health, the continuing uproar
over the publication of *Cain*, and an unfortunate imbroglio
with the Italian authorities, the 'Pisan Affray' − all contributed
to make the first half of 1822 particularly difficult and unhappy.
Byron was also occupied with *The Deformed Transformed*, the
last of his verse plays, begun at roughly the same time as Canto
VI, and destined to shadow the remainder of *Don Juan*, like
a dark twin, until his death in Greece left it, too, incomplete.
Byron was almost certainly hampered as well, however, by
problems which confronted him from within the poem. He
seems to have found, in particular, that he now wanted to
hurry the Gulbeyaz episode to a conclusion, making it far
more perfunctory than originally designed.

   The absence of any overall scheme for *Don Juan* was something Byron had insisted upon almost querulously in early state-
ments. On 12 August 1819 he informed his worried publisher
that 'I *have* no plan − I *had* no plan − but I had or have
materials' (BLJ VI. 207). The narrator, while comically glancing
over his shoulder from time to time at the requirements of
epic form, nonetheless maintains a pretence of randomness
throughout. In Canto IX, he slyly informs the reader that

> I ne'er decide what I shall say, and this I call
>   Much too poetical. Men should know why
> They write, and for what end; but, note or text,
> I never know the word which will come next.
>
> So on I ramble, now and then narrating,
>   Now pondering.   (41−2)

A similar insouciance continues to flaunt itself in stanza 19 of Canto XV. It is clear, of course, even before the watershed of Canto VI, that whatever his uncertainty as to the future course of the story, Byron was always acutely conscious of what he had *already* written, and of the need to take this into account when devising further episodes. This retrospective awareness, far more than a matter of simple narrative consistency, as the Raucocanti interlude alone makes plain, means that whatever Byron said about the absence of premeditation, *Don Juan* was always purposefully cumulative in terms of its own past. It is not just that its hero alters as a result of his experiences; the poem steadily thickens in texture, unlike Defoe's *Moll Flanders*, or a picaresque novel by Smollett.

There is evidence, moreover, that after Canto V Byron did begin to look further and further ahead, while still retaining considerable freedom of manœuvre. Judging from what he told Murray in a letter of 16 February 1821, and repeated to Captain Medwin early in 1822, Juan's death in the aftermath of the French Revolution had now become a fixed terminus. What remained imponderable was the amount of time and the variety of circumstance required to conduct him, and the poem, to that resolution. Byron apparently told Medwin early in 1822 that 'if' he resumed work on *Don Juan*, he would have the sultana and Juan escape from the seraglio and travel to Russia together. There, 'if Juan's passion cools, and I don't know what to do with the lady, I shall make her die of the plague'. Juan was then to become 'man-mistress' to Catherine the Great, and go to England on a diplomatic mission, taking with him a 'girl whom he shall have rescued during one of his northern campaigns, who shall be in love with him, and he not with her'. He does not mention Ismail, and yet in the poem as written, this episode occupies all of Cantos VII and VIII.

Byron obviously enjoyed detailing 'Juanna's' night in the harem, a lone man among more than one thousand concubines and their governess, the 'Mistress of the Maids'. Purportedly slaves of love, but woefully starved of the thing itself, the inmates half-consciously intuit his hidden maleness, contending with each other when it is discovered that the newcomer's

unexpected arrival finds them one bed short for the privilege
of sharing their own. Back on the slave-ship, when the pairing
of captives by sex left one odd woman and one man, Juan,
chained to the fair Italian, had successfully resisted temptation.
When the situation repeats itself, in the bed of that 'sleepy
Venus', Dudù (VI.42), Haidée is forgotten as Juan surrenders
to desire. Byron writes with comic sparkle and *élan* about the
sympathies and little rivalries of the seraglio, without forgetting
its underlying sadness, about Dudù's sudden scream in the night,
and the wonderfully Freudian dream she invents to explain it
and prevent the lover she has so unexpectedly acquired from
being removed. The fun of the whole episode is enhanced by
its frame: that stultifying nuptial chamber where Gulbeyaz
endures the embraces of her wedded lord, and then rises from
a joyless bed to discover that Juan has not slept alone. When
the canto ends, she has just summoned the guilty pair and
instructed Baba to arrange for a boat 'by the secret portal's
side' (113) to bear them to destruction.

Byron went through the motions at this point of tantalizing
readers as to the outcome: 'whether / Gulbeyaz shewed them
both commiseration, / Or got rid of the parties altogether',
being things 'the turning of a hair or feather / May settle'
(119). Meanwhile, he announced, a digression being perfectly
in order, his Muse would 'take a little touch at warfare' (120).
In the event, this 'digression' not only became the substance
of the next two cantos, but crowded out any explanation of
how Juan escaped from Constantinople, let alone the fate of
the woman once described as the poem's 'third heroine'. The
little party of travellers surprised at twilight in Canto VII by
Suwarrow's cossacks consists of Juan, his English friend, and
two anonymous Turkish ladies who are said (with their atten-
dant Baba) to have aided the men's flight. One of these women
is presumably Dudù. The identity of the other remains a
mystery, but it cannot be the outraged and fierce Gulbeyaz.
Not only does the sultana never reach Russia as once planned;
she appears instead to have been summarily abandoned, and
forgotten about, in Constantinople. As for Juan's weeping
female companions, once they have been despatched to the

temporary safety of the baggage train, they and Baba vanish too: dumped from the story as unceremoniously as if they had indeed been sewn into sacks and lowered into the Bosphorus. Apart from Juan himself, the only member of this group so briefly glimpsed in whom Byron retained any interest under the new circumstances of his poem was the Englishman: a previous *alter ego* for both narrator and hero whose status he was about, quite drastically, to change.

Outside the walls of Ismail, Juan's acquaintance returns to his trade, that of 'those butchers in large business, your mercenary soldiery' (BLJ IX.191). As soon as he does so, Byron, who loathed these men, immediately cancels this character's partial association with the narrator. Here he names the Englishman at last, Johnson, thus linking him unequivocally (the name, once introduced, becomes a constant) with Juan alone. The young Spaniard is not yet so hardened: the fate of Leila, the little Muslim orphan he rescues from the cossacks, will matter more to him than his share of the plunder. Yet, after some initial hesitation, he finds it all too easy to emulate the behaviour of his older friend, hacking and maiming in the pursuit of 'glory' other human beings who are merely trying to defend their homes and families from destruction by an invading army. The one real difference is that whereas the experienced Johnson retreats strategically when a position becomes too dangerous, Juan impetuously rushes on, without noticing that he no longer has a regiment around him. Their paired names now point to a relationship from which the narrator has withdrawn.

Byron must always have known that his perspective on Johnson was going to shift as soon as he returned to being a soldier in foreign pay. There would have been no point, otherwise, in so carefully keeping back his name. The mention to Medwin, however, of Juan's 'northern campaigns' suggests that Turkish Ismail, on the Danube, may not originally have figured in Byron's mind as the scene of his poem's major attack upon wars of conquest. It came to do so, probably, because of both his eagerness now to shed the Gulbeyaz plot before Russia rather than after, and the effect on him of the Marquis de Castelnau's *Essai sur l'histoire ancienne et moderne de la Nouvelle Russie*. In that work, published in Paris in 1820, the siege of Ismail, in all its horror, was described with exactly the kind of detailed attention to facts Byron required by a historian whose complacent celebration of war in general, and this Russian victory in particular, he found infuriating.

In the epigraph, taken from Shakespeare's *Twelfth Night* (II.iii), which he appended to Cantos VI–VIII ('Dost thou think, because thou art virtuous, there shall be no more Cakes and Ale?' – 'Yes, by St Anne; and Ginger shall be hot i' the mouth too!'), Byron deployed the voice of comedy (Sir Toby Belch and Feste the jester) to round on a reading public now personified as Malvolio, that conspicuously self-satisfied hypocrite and prig. The prose Preface he provided for the three new cantos was blistering in its attack upon the memory of Castlereagh, whose recent suicide in no way allowed Byron to forget his policies: 'as to lamenting his death, it will be time enough when Ireland has ceased to mourn for his birth'. He also extended the epigraph's assault upon 'cant', adducing Voltaire's comments about the flight of modesty and morality to the lips once they have ceased to govern human hearts, against those who had professed to find the earlier cantos of *Don Juan* blasphemous and indecent.

So far as Murray was concerned, the new cantos, which reached him in the autumn of 1822, enforced a parting of the ways: 'I declare to you they were so outrageously shocking that I would not publish them if you were to give me your Estate – Title and Genius – For Heaven's sake revise them.' But Byron, who had informed Moore on 8 August that it was 'necessary, in the present clash of philosophy and tyranny, to throw away the scabbard', not only refused to alter what he had written, but asked for the return of those stanzas attacking Wellington which had prudently been removed from Canto III. These he reworked and placed defiantly at the beginning of Canto IX. Not only Cantos VI–VIII, but the remainder of *Don Juan* would henceforth be published by the radical John Hunt.

Dudù's 'dream' in the harem, together with the sexual

innuendo informing Cantos VI and IX throughout, must have struck Murray as reprehensible enough. Equally alarming were the savagely anti-royalist, anti-war convictions which dominate the Ismail cantos: Byron's merciless assault on imperialism, militarism, heroes, glory and the concern for men of rank while ordinary soldiers die unheeded. He told Kinnaird that the siege episode was written 'in the style of the Storm in the 2nd C[ant]o ... with much philosophy – and satire upon heroes and despots and the present false state of politics and society' (BLJ IX. 196). Ismail does resemble the shipwreck in scale, and also in its portrayal of human behaviour under extreme conditions. Again, there are a few redeeming instances of courage, primarily among the defenders of the city (the old Pacha, the Tartar Khan and his five sons), of compassion (Juan's rescue of Leila), or consummate professional skill (Suwarrow drilling his recruits), even if the last is directed to abhorrent ends. The overall tone, however, of Cantos VII and VIII is very different from that of Canto II. The narrator is angry: an anger all the more lethal and effective for being partnered by savage humour, and for being kept under tight control.

Most of the attitudes informing the Ismail cantos now seem so transparently right that it requires an effort of imagination to understand how dismaying they would have been for those English readers who had admired *Childe Harold*, coming to them as they did in the aftermath of Waterloo and the resulting national self-congratulation. Byron at one point alludes to Wordsworth's 'Ode: The Morning of the Day Appointed for a General Thanksgiving. January 18, 1816', in which the older poet had managed to claim that the Creator's

> ... most dreaded instrument
> In working out a pure intent,
> Is man arrayed for mutual slaughter;
> Yea, *Carnage is thy daughter!*

'Perhaps as pretty a pedigree for Murder as ever was found out by Garter King at Arms', Byron noted sardonically, and proceeded to savage it in *Don Juan*: ' "Carnage" (so Wordsworth

tells you) "is God's daughter:" / If *he* speak truth, she is
Christ's sister, and / Just now behaved as in the Holy Land'
(VIII. 9). Wordsworth opined on more than one occasion that
the author of *Don Juan* was insane. Nevertheless, as Ruskin
was the first to notice, when Wordsworth revised the 'Ode' in
1843, dividing it into two, he deleted the lines Byron had singled
out. Their omission left poems which, in their full-throated
celebration of monarchy, the Holy Alliance, and England's
divine mandate to preserve her own and Europe's political
status quo, Byron would still have found insufferable. By that
time, however, Wordsworth's sentence of perpetual exile passed
on any 'ungrateful Son' of Britain 'Who can forget thy prowess'
had come to seem oddly prophetic.

'In royalty's vast arms'

Mary Shelley, Byron's amanuensis for Cantos VI–XVI of
Don Juan, sometimes made minor changes in the authorial
manuscripts she copied. On only one occasion, however,
did she flatly refuse to write out a portion of the text: the
sodomy pun (lines 601–2 of Canto VIII) at the expense of the
recently disgraced bishop of Clogher. Byron was obliged to
enter it himself in the fair copy. Whatever Mary Wollstone-
craft's daughter may have thought of the subsequent lines about
those 'widows of forty' in the ransacked city who were 'heard
to wonder in the din / ... Wherefore the ravishing did not
begin!' (VIII. 132), she reproduced them without demur. This
ancient joke (Byron had used it years before, in 'The Devil's
Drive', and it did not originate with him) is one of the few
instances of a passage in *Don Juan* likely to offend more readers
today than when it was first published. The joke is not, however, a piece of gratuitous misogyny.

In *The Deformed Transformed*, written concurrently with
Don Juan VI–XVI, Byron treated the prospect of Olimpia's
rape by drunken soldiers during the sack of Rome realistically
and with entire seriousness. The widows and the 'waning
prude[s]' (st. 131) of Ismail, by contrast, are caricature figures
in a comic tradition that goes back to Aristophanes, and to

Fletcher's Chloë in *The Faithful Shepherdess* (1608), who reminds herself when lost on a dark night that 'No one can ravish me, I am so willing.' Byron even forgets for the moment that these are Muslim, not Western, women. He introduces them, in part, because here, towards the end of the war cantos, the characteristically mixed tone of *Don Juan* is in jeopardy: ' 'tis not / My cue for any time to be terrific', the narrator reminds both himself and his readers in stanza 89 of Canto VIII. Human beings do appalling things to each other, but the poem needs to remember that, even in a ransacked city, human life is still 'checquered' with 'good, and bad, and worse, alike prolific / Of melancholy merriment'. The reflection serves to introduce, first, Juan's rescue of the child Leila – an isolated good deed the narrator sardonically predicts his Pharisaical readers will call ' "quite refreshing" ' (VIII.90) – then the heroic last stand of the Tartar Khan, and finally, by way of the longing ladies of Ismail, a reminder of something, already adumbrated in the seraglio, which the Russian canto is about to address directly: the connection between war and certain suspect kinds of sexuality or, as the narrator puts it, 'homicide and harlotry' (VII.37).

As a combination, love and war, epic themes usually inter-twined since Homer in ways that glorify both, receive short shrift at Byron's hands. Not by accident were the gilded bronze portals sealing off the sultan's harem in Canto V said to be decorated with carved warriors 'battling furiously' (86), with captives led in triumph, and with the slain. The sultan himself, rising from Gulbeyaz's bed, irritably contemplates recent Russian victories over the Turks, 'in Catherine's reign, whom glory still adores / As greatest of all sovereigns and w----s' (VI.92). The grandmother of an important partner in the Holy Alliance, 'grand legitimate Alexander' (VI.93), Catherine the Great repelled Byron on a number of counts. The essentially trivial but (in its consequences) catastrophic imperialism of this widowed despot, nearing sixty, existed in uneasy conjunction with a sexual insatiability in which 'her climacteric teased her like her teens' (X.47). Catherine's stable of lovers was not a mere rumour. It had received detailed attention in several

historical accounts of her reign — including William Tooke's
Life of Catherine II, Empress of Russia (1800) — one of the
books Byron consulted. Scarcely a stranger himself to
promiscuity, what he found distasteful about Catherine was
not so much the number of her partners as her reduction of
them to sexual machines, together with the connivance in it all
of a sycophantic and corrupt court.

On the whole, Canto IX and its successor — at least up
to stanza 49 when the hero and his little ward depart for
England — have been the least admired sections of *Don Juan*.
Perhaps because he himself had never set foot in Russia, Byron
makes no real attempt to re-create life in St Petersburg as he
had at Seville, Constantinople, or on Haidée's island. Narrative
is reduced to a handful of disconnected snapshots: Juan and
Leila jolting in a *kibitka* along the road to the capitol; Juan
kneeling for a seemingly interminable moment to present his
despatch while the entire court holds its breath as Catherine's
jubilation at the news of a city taken, and thirty thousand
slain, is superseded by her undisguised lust for the handsome
messenger who brought it; a blur of dances, revels and ready
money, of 'waste, and haste, and glare, and gloss, and glitter'
(X. 26); and finally that incapacitating illness which forces the
empress to send her young lover away to travel for his health
— and to replace him within two days. The story intermittently
flashes into and then out of sight almost as though it had now
become a digression from the main matter of the cantos: the
narrator's brooding reflections on death, sexuality, politics
and (increasingly) his own past.

The bawdy and innuendo of the harem episode in Cantos V
and VI had been light-hearted and playful. Here, in Russia,
the narrator's tone is wryly disabused as he contemplates 'What
a curious way / The whole thing is of clothing souls in clay'
(IX. 75). Outrageous phallic jokes mingle with what Hamlet
punningly called 'country matters', as Byron suddenly concen-
trates on the anatomical and physiological basis of 'love':
orgasm, erections, vaginal secretions, the effects of the meno-
pause. That Murray should have severed his connection with
poetry whose meaning, beneath its mock innocence and

circumlocution, is so unmistakable seems less surprising than John Hunt daring to print it at all. Byron adopts the attitude he does partly because it is in keeping with the degrading nature of Juan's fourth affair: a matter of 'self-love' (IX.68) on the young man's part and sheer appetite on Catherine's. The character of the relationship is epitomized from its start by Miss Protasoff, 'Named from her mystic office "l'Eprouveuse" ' (84), whisking Juan off to submit to a physical examination and demonstrate his fitness to oust the current favourite among the empress' 'standing army' (78) of six-footers from his place 'In royalty's vast arms' and bed (X.37). The cantos are also influenced, however, by Byron's brooding awareness that he was now approaching thirty-five, Dante's 'horrid equinox' (X.27) of human existence, that his youth was over, and old age and death within view.

Byron clearly intended the first ten stanzas of Canto IX, addressed to Wellington, to be read as a kind of proem, distinct from the main body of the canto. When IX properly begins, at stanza 11, it finds the narrator (metaphorically) in a graveyard, contemplating Yorick's grinning skull. From that meditation springs much of what follows. *The Tempest* had presided over the idyll of the island in Canto II, giving place only when things went wrong to reminders of *Hamlet. Hamlet*, however, controls Canto IX throughout. The narrator is driven with tell-tale frequency back to Shakespeare's text: 'To be or not to be' (14, 16), the special providence in the sparrow's fall (19), the 'Courtier's kibes' (35), 'The time is out of joint' (41), the strangeness of man, that infinite piece of work (64), or 'the Herald Mercury' of the prince's rebuke to Gertrude (66). He even imitates Polonius, slyly, at stanza 36: 'I have forgotten what I meant to say.' Such particularized references, however, are less important than the penumbra of concerns they focus.

In 1822 Byron was deeply worried – like Hamlet, although for different reasons – about his failure to prove himself a man of action. As early as 23 August 1819, he had told Hobhouse that 'I feel & feel it bitterly – that a man should not consume his life at the side and on the bosom – of a woman... and that this CiSisbean existence is to be condemned. – But

I have neither the strength of mind to break my chain, nor the insensibility which would deaden its weight' (BLJ VI.214). Although his involvement with the Italian Carbonari movement gave political purpose to his existence for a time, the planned revolution fizzled out. Byron's thoughts increasingly turned towards Greece, ever more restive under foreign rule, only to find that his constitutional disinclination to uproot himself was compounded by the difficulty of abandoning Teresa, 'a woman who has left her husband for a man, and the weakness of one's own heart' (BLJ VIII.214). Not until July 1823 did he finally set out. Meanwhile, his dissatisfaction with himself and his way of life found a vent in *Don Juan*.

Teresa was considerably younger than Byron, and in no sense the dominant partner of the two. Yet he could see, and did not relish, a connection between 'the Imperial Favourite's Condition' (IX.52) and his own function as the countess's 'Cavalier Servente', even drawing attention to it in the poem. His bawdy references to that 'gate of Life and Death ... / Whence is our exit and our entrance' (IX.55), source of men's rises and falls, together with his sardonic bemusement at its power, derive both from Juan's particular circumstances in this canto and Byron's own. The narrator's metaphysical speculations, like Hamlet's, tend to terminate in self-mockery, not only because of his fundamental scepticism and distrust of systems, but because they keep entangling themselves with the tragi-comedy of sexual desire.

In the graveyard Hamlet had found himself overwhelmed by his past: that of the child carried piggy-back by Yorick the jester in the court of a different king. In Canto X, as he prepares to send Juan and Leila to the England he had not seen himself for almost seven years, Byron's own past enters the poem for the first time wearing the guise of unabashed nostalgia. His mind goes back not only to *English Bards and Scotch Reviewers*, that brilliant satirical indiscretion committed when he was 'juvenile and curly' (X.19), and the quarrels it occasioned, but to his childhood in Scotland: 'Scotch plaids, Scotch snoods, the blue hills, and clear streams, / The Dee, the Don, Balgounie's Brig's *black wall*, / All my boy feelings'

(X. 18). When Juan and Leila in their imperial coach arrive at 'the castellated Rhine' (X. 61), they begin to reverse Byron's own itinerary, as described in Canto III of *Childe Harold*, when he left England for the last time in the spring of 1816. From the moment that the chalk cliff-faces of Dover become visible from the Channel, the narrator's voice undergoes a significant alteration: one that will effectively set the long last section of *Don Juan* slightly apart from the rest of the poem.

'The thousand happy few'

Juan's Russian sojourn may have left him a little blasé about women ('his heart had got a tougher rind', XII. 81), but where European politics are concerned he is still touchingly naive. Catherine's envoy arrives at Dover persuaded that England is 'Freedom's chosen station' (XI. 9): a constitutional monarchy shaming other nations where justice, morality, social order and freedom of speech all flourish to the heart's desire, and though the cost of living is high, society's great wealth is distributed to all the deserving. This complacent view, shared by many Tories at the time, Byron rapidly reduces to tatters. Even before Juan, pausing on Shooter's Hill to admire the great dusky panorama of London stretched out below, has his reverie and illusions shattered by the 'freeborn sounds' of ' "Damn your eyes! your money or your life!" ' (XI. 11, 10) and is obliged to kill a not wholly unsympathetic member of England's criminal classes in self-defence, the narrator has prepared for and already undercut his hero's enthusiasm.

Here, as throughout the poem, he keeps before the reader something to which Juan remains oblivious: England's 'decaying fame' (X. 66), her tarnished reputation as the jailor of European nations struggling to be free, and the hypocrisy and cant riddling her social, political and religious institutions. No longer confined to digressions and asides, Byron's reflections on England and (more particularly) the English upper classes become, in these last cantos, the substance of *Don Juan*. The satire is mordant, and yet pulling against it are impulses of a different kind. As Juan's carriage rattles out of '*dear* Dover'

(X.69) *en route* to London — 'On with the horses! Off to
Canterbury! / Tramp, tramp, o'er pebble, and splash, splash,
thro' puddle' (71) — it acquires an extra passenger: Byron
himself, returning in his imagination to cloudy skies, green
fields, English turnpike roads and, in the metropolis itself, a
whole world left behind. In Seville, during the shipwreck, on
Haidée's island, at Constantinople and Ismail, even to some
extent in Russia, the narrator had been genuinely interested in
how his hero reacted to the surroundings and experiences provided for him by the poem. In London, by contrast, Juan's
responses are so heavily overlaid by the narrator's own that
it becomes virtually impossible to see this city (except in flashes)
as an inquisitive foreigner actually might.

So, on Shooter's Hill, Juan's awed appreciation of London's
'mighty mass of brick, and smoke, and shipping' slides almost
at once into a mocking description of St Paul's 'huge, dun
cupola, like a foolscap crown / On a fool's head' (X.82),
inconceivable as the reaction of the young Spaniard. Here, at
the beginning of the English section, the narrator abruptly
pulls himself up: 'But Juan saw not this' (83). Once again, he
tries to look at London through the eyes of an outsider, someone for whom even her choking pall of smoke indicates 'The
wealth of worlds', only to suffer a parenthetical relapse: '(a
wealth of tax and paper)'. Once Juan has actually entered the
city, Byron for the most part abandons this pretence. At
Norman Abbey, even though he intrudes at one moment into
his own fiction, sitting down at the Amundeville's dinner table
next to that 'very powerful Parson, Peter Pith, / The loudest
wit I e'er was deafened with' (XVI.81), narrative, and with it
Juan's independence, will be restored. Throughout Cantos XI,
XII and XIII, however, the narrator's need to re-live his
personal past, while not losing sight of the actual moment in
which he is writing, virtually elbows Juan's fictional present
off the stage.

Occasionally, Byron remembers that the year is supposed
to be 1791, that in Parliament 'Grey was not arrived, and
Chatham gone' (XII.82), or that the future George IV, a
personable and slender prince, was still the hope of the Whig

party, and 'A finished gentleman from top to toe' (84). Essentially, however, the London he depicts is that of his own youth and years of fame, between the publication of *Childe Harold* I and II in 1812, and his departure from England in 1816: one in which Charles, second Earl Grey, was eloquently opposing repressive legislation, the society frequenting Holland, Devonshire and the other great Whig houses was heady and permissive, gas lighting was newly ablaze in the West End, Sheridan, Lady Melbourne, and the 'dandies' flourished, and the Prince Regent, although he had already abandoned both his wife and his former Whig allies, at least had not swelled into that embarrassingly 'great George' who later tipped the scales at twenty stone (VIII. 126). To this glittering Regency world the narrator looks back from the vantage-point of 1823, and finds that − like his own youth − it has bewilderingly disappeared. The so-called *ubi sunt* ('where are they?') passage (XI. 76−85) is one of the most stunning in the poem, not least because it contrives to be at the same time wonderfully specific in its wry lament for a particular modern society and as timeless as Villon's 'Où sont les neiges d'antan?' in his 'Ballade des dames du temps jadis' (*Le Grand Testament*, 1489).

Byron's extended meditation on ephemerality follows (and in a sense is generated by) a particularly vicious stanza describing 'the life of a young noble' (XI. 74). Often singled out (originally by A. B. England, more recently by Bernard Beatty) as an attempt to imitate, in *ottava rima*, the manner of Pope, the unequivocal logic and tightly disciplined verbal pattern manifested in this stanza are essentially Augustan:

> They are young, but know not youth − it is anticipated;
>   Handsome but wasted, rich without a sou;
> Their vigour in a thousand arms is dissipated;
>   Their cash comes *from*, their wealth goes *to* a Jew;
> Both senates see their nightly votes participated
>   Between the tyrant's and the tribunes' crew;
> And having voted, dined, drank, gamed, and whored,
> The family vault receives another lord.

(75)

This little 'biography' may be horrific, an unsparing delineation of futility and disorder the more depressing because it is so petty; the verse itself, with its nicely balanced antitheses ('Handsome but wasted, rich without a sou', '*from ... to*', ''tyrant's' weighed against 'tribunes' ') and its epigrammatic couplet, is confident and single-minded in its satiric conviction. A control at once moral and aesthetic dictates the order of the verbs in the penultimate line, the crescendo from 'voted' to 'whored' registering like five deathly hammer-blows, each more powerful than the one before, which nail down the coffin-lid of the young lord.

Although intermittently visible in *Don Juan*, this is a style Byron rarely can (or wishes to) sustain. In this particular instance, he departs from it in the very next stanza and, in doing so, suddenly reveals the extent to which 75, for all its surface poise, had harboured all along the seeds of its own destruction:

> 'Where is the world', cries Young, 'at *eighty*? Where
>   The world in which a man was born?' Alas!
> Where is the world of *eight* years past? *'Twas there* —
>   I look for it — 'tis gone, a Globe of Glass!
> Cracked, shivered, vanished, scarcely gazed on, ere
>   A silent change dissolves the glittering mass.
> Statesmen, chiefs, orators, queens, patriots, kings,
> And dandies, all are gone on the wind's wings.
>
>   (76)

The satiric force of 75 depends to a large extent upon the apparent impersonality of the poet: neutral, dispassionate, eminently rational, speaking from a position far above the vice and folly he condemns. This detachment crumbles completely in 76, and with it — as Byron begins to speak with his own wayward, interrogative, and significantly more generous, untidy voice — the polished Augustanism of the verse. As a result the reader is impelled back to 75 in order to discover some reason for a change of style and mood so drastic and, at first sight, unmotivated.

Stanza 76 retrospectively transforms 75 by uncovering the extent to which it was really tormentedly autobiographical. The '*eight* years past' of 76 looks back quite specifically to

1814. In doing so it summons up, inevitably, Byron's own period of dissipation as a 'young nobleman': sexual adventurer, gambler in London clubs, himself 'handsome but wasted', seriously handicapped by debts incurred through an injudicious resort to Jewish money-lenders – 'In my young days they lent me cash that way, / Which I found very troublesome to pay' (II. 65). In Canto I of *Don Juan*, written in 1818, the poet (aged thirty) had already commented ruefully on his prematurely greying looks and reflected that 'I / Have squander'd my whole summer while 'twas May' (I. 213). The real gloss, however, on stanza 75's 'They are young, but know not youth – it is anticipated' is provided by a passage in 'Detached Thoughts', the journal Byron began in October 1821: 'My passions were developed very early – so early – that few would believe me – if I were to state the period – and the facts which accompanied it. – Perhaps this was one of the reasons which caused the anticipated melancholy of my thoughts – having anticipated life' (BLJ IX. 40).

The Byron 'family vault' in Nottinghamshire was not going to claim the author of stanza 75 until 1824, nor had his existence (despite periods of despondency and frustration) ever been as aimless and trivial as the one satirized. His awareness, however, that in certain important respects the 'young noble' so sweepingly dismissed might be identified with one of his earlier selves serves to trigger off a characteristic reaction – both emotional and stylistic – against that dismissal. Stanza 76 is not only unabashedly personal but is also associative, conversational and tolerant, indeed nostalgic, as its predecessor was not. After telescoping Young's placid ruminations in *Resignation* (1762) about the alterations wrought by the passing of eighty years into a feverish matter of 'eight', the narrator catapults his reader onto the battlements at Elsinore. For a split second he sees the past as Horatio, Bernardo and Marcellus do Old Hamlet's ghost, something of quicksilver insubstantiality, fleeting and ungraspable (' 'Tis here!' / ' 'Tis here! / 'Tis gone!'), before transforming it into a 'Globe of Glass' which not only shatters but is instantly metamorphosed into glittering snow, dissolving silently, 'scarcely gazed on', as soon as it strikes the ground. Byron liked to annoy Leigh Hunt in Italy by pretending to find Spenser unreadable, but here he was almost certainly remembering Merlin's 'glassie globe' in Book III of *The Faerie Queene*, an enchanted crystal which showed 'What ever thing was in the world contaynd, / Betwixt the lowest earth and heavens hight, / So that it to the looker appertaynd.' The stanza incorporates one of Byron's most haunting and brilliant 'chains of thought': the evanescence which is its subject reflected in the rapidity with which deliberately half-realized images crowd and jostle for place, without allowing the reader time to protest that there seem to be few, if any, logical links between them. Nothing could be further from the reasoned solidity of 75 than the verse movement of 76, continually collapsing in on itself, through which Byron records the disappearance of an entire social world. Even the couplet, declining to be epigrammatic, sedulously refuses to order its heterogeneous sequence of seven nouns: 'Statesmen, chiefs, orators, queens, patriots, kings, / And dandies, all are gone on the wind's wings.' The reader who grasps at 'kings' as a climax of the same kind as 'whored' is quickly disabused when 'dandies' appears, in the next line, as the real end of this sequence – and also, perhaps, a little surprised by the sadness, the note of genuine regret denied to 'kings', with which its ambiguous position (culmination or mere afterthought?) manages to invest it.

Behind the detailed reconstruction of a Regency world in the *ubi sunt* stanzas, and in the last cantos of *Don Juan* generally, lies the same retrospective impulse that had already impelled Byron in 1818 to write, and give to Moore for safe-keeping, his ill-fated 'Memoirs'. The pusillanimity and petty jealousies of his friends ensured that the prose autobiography was burned after his death – a fate most of them would gladly have wished on *Don Juan* as well. The poem differs from what is known about the 'Memoirs' in avoiding, or at least blurring, the out-lines of specific personalities. Lady Pinchbeck, for instance, the dowager 'high in high circles, gentle in her own' (XII. 48), to whom Juan entrusts the education of little Leila, is based in part on Lady Melbourne, but she would not have thanked

him for the association with sham gold, nor did Byron intend
it to apply to the friend he had mourned sincerely as 'the best
& kindest & ablest female I ever knew — old or young' (BLJ
VI. 34). His concern in the London cantos is less with individuals
than with the manners and morals of 'the Great World, —
which being interpreted / Meaneth the West or worst end of a
city, / And about twice two thousand people bred / By no
means to be very wise or witty' (XI. 45). Its sexual mores
interest him especially, above all the bizarre customs — as
outlandish as anything to be found further east — associated
with that thriving commercial enterprise, the marriage market.

Although the narrator can be savagely condemnatory (as in
his thumbnail sketch of the 'young noble'), the characteristic
tone of the London section is mixed: appreciative and satiric
in equal measure, and frequently modulating from one to the
other with disconcerting speed:

> Then dress, then dinner, then awakes the world!
>   Then glare the lamps, then whirl the wheels, then roar
> Through street and square fast flashing chariots, hurled
>   Like harnessed meteors; then along the floor
> Chalk mimics painting; then festoons are twirled;
>   Then roll the brazen thunders of the door,
> Which opens to the thousand happy few
> An earthly Paradise of 'Or Molu'.
>
> (XI. 67)

Like pinchbeck but more substantial, ormolu is an alloy of
copper, zinc or tin masquerading as gold. Fashionable as a
material for clocks, much used to ornament Regency furniture,
it epitomizes a society in which success depends upon hypocrisy
and caution and the narrator can knowingly advise his hero to
'be / Not what you *seem*, but always what you *see*' (XI. 86):
counsel which, investigated closely, can be seen to imply not
merely politic concealment, but an actual erosion of the
integrity of the self.

It is in the context of fictitious gold — whether in the form
of pinchbeck, ormolu, paper money, or the credit extended by
tradesmen to society beauties for finery that will be paid for,
ultimately, by the husband it ensnares — that the narrator's

long mock-encomium at the beginning of Canto XII on the miser's more solid treasures, ingots and diamonds, coins and gold rouleaus, the cash that 'rules Love the ruler, on his own/ High ground' (14), demands to be read. The younger Byron had stubbornly refused, even when in serious financial straits, to accept payment for his poems. Although he continued, in Italy, quietly to give away money to anyone who needed it, his attitude towards his literary profits underwent a radical change. In letters to Murray and others, he took to haggling fiercely over terms for his new works, including the successive instalments of *Don Juan*, taking a perverse pleasure now in caricaturing himself as the most grasping and niggardly of men. An attitude already adumbrated in Canto I ('So for a good old gentlemanly vice, / I think I must take up with avarice', 216), it becomes calculatedly outrageous in Canto XII. Triggered off (as usual) by the narrator's search for something to replace the lost illusions and pleasures of his youth, it also excoriates a society dominated by financial considerations which tries, dishonestly, to pretend otherwise.

Inevitably, re-visiting London impelled Byron to contrast his former popularity as a writer with the obloquy showered upon his recent works, including *Don Juan*: a poem 'as much the subject of attack / As ever yet was any work sublime' (XI. 90). It also reminded him that the meteoric career of Napoleon was in those years plummeting towards its final eclipse. The death in 1822 of Byron's detested mother-in-law had obliged him, for legal reasons, to add the family name 'Noel' to his own. This, to his amusement, gave him the same initials as Napoleon Bonaparte, and is likely to have prompted his rueful self-description as the erstwhile 'grand Napoleon of the realms of rhyme' (XI. 55), a poet whose recent disasters – *Don Juan*, *Marino Faliero* and *Cain* – corresponded to Moscow, Leipzig and Waterloo: the three battles which, between 1812 and 1815, had cost his namesake an empire of a different kind. The comparison implies a similar importance on the world stage and, indeed, throughout the English cantos Byron's quiet confidence in the worth of *Don Juan* as a whole is unmistakable, as is his awareness that these latest additions constituted (as VI had done before) yet another fresh start.

At the end of Canto XII, the narrator suddenly announces that the entire poem up to this point has been an 'introduction', and that the main body of the book — 'of a different construction' (87) — is only now about to begin. Another joke at the expense of the 'atrocious reader', who is threatened with a whole canto on 'Political Economy', it nonetheless contains a measure of truth. Behind the wanderings of Juan, the essentially episodic nature of the poem before it comes to rest in England, there had always lurked the picaresque adventures of heroes such as Smollett's Roderick Random and Peregrine Pickle, Swift's Gulliver, or Fielding's Joseph Andrews and Tom Jones. Byron's stance as narrator, simultaneously creator and commentator on his own creation, digressive, ruminative and wryly comic, owes much throughout to Fielding's stage management of *Tom Jones* — another work counterpoising a naive, uncomplicated protagonist with a sophisticated, sceptical and ultimately dominant authorial presence. It is also indebted to the rambling, associative voice which narrates Sterne's *Tristram Shandy*, with its intense artistic self-consciousness and whimsical fluctuations of mood. It is in the English cantos, however, particularly in the last three, that *Don Juan* is most strikingly like a novel.

According to his 'Memorandum' of 1807, the young Byron had by that year already devoured some 'thousands' of novels. Even allowing for youthful exaggeration, it is clear that from an early age he made his way through massive amounts of prose fiction. The great English novels of the eighteenth century (Richardson excluded) probably left the deepest impression, but he also ranged widely among foreign authors and the works of his own contemporaries. Cervantes' *Don Quixote*, the subject in Canto XIII of a four-stanza digression on the failure of all idealisms, is the only novel discussed at any length in *Don Juan*. It needs to be remembered, however, that during his years in Italy Byron read and re-read Scott's Waverley series (Juan's passivity may owe something to Scott's heroes), and that packets of new books were continually sent out to

him from England. They included 'society' novels such as
Caroline Lamb's *Glenarvon* (1816), which contained an infamous portrait of Byron himself, and Thomas Love Peacock's
country house satires. Byron is said to have enjoyed Peacock's
caricature of him as the gloomy and self-dramatizing Mr
Cypress in *Nightmare Abbey* (1818) — 'Sir, I have quarrelled
with my wife; and a man who has quarrelled with his wife is
absolved from all duty to his country. I have written an ode
to tell the people as much, and they may take it as they list.'
More important was the influence of Peacock's incongruous,
opinionated assemblies upon the gathering of guests at Byron's
Norman Abbey. Here, for the first time in the poem, the
narrator begins to construct a complex and identifiably
novelistic plot: one involving Juan's simultaneous relationship
with three very different upper-class women, not to mention
a ghost.

'The fair most fatal Juan ever met'

From the moment that Juan espies the English coast from the
Channel packet, the focus of the poem steadily narrows:
diminishing from Dover, Canterbury, and the sprawl of London
viewed from Shooter's Hill to the West End's meticulously
observed 'twice two thousand people' of fashion (XI. 45), and
then the claustrophobic autumn house party at Norman Abbey.
There Lord and Lady Amundeville assemble thirty-three guests
and receive a miscellany of callers. Norman Abbey itself, with
its lake, cascade, Gothic fountain and great ruined arch, still
retaining undefaced its image of 'the Virgin Mother of the
God-born child' (XIII. 61), is unmistakably Newstead, Byron's
ancestral home near Nottingham, which in 1817 he had finally
sold. It is a Newstead grander and in far better repair than the
original: architecturally more distinguished, filled not only
with a galaxy of family portraits, but with paintings by Titian,
Rembrandt, Caravaggio and Claude that the Byrons never
possessed. The ancient oaks surrounding it had been felled by
the poet's lunatic great-uncle before his own birth. Byron's deep
affection for this place — he had resided there intermittently

between 1808 and his marriage in 1815 – is in striking contrast to his distaste for most of its aristocratic inhabitants: the guests he depicts sauntering through its galleries and halls, idly turning the pages of books in the library, eating their way through epic dinners, or victimizing (Byron hated blood sports) the foxes, the partridges, the pheasants and the trout.

Cupidity had characterized that 'microcosm on stilts / Yclept the Great World' (XII. 56) through which Juan moved, gracefully but only half-comprehending, in London. Neither cash nor the ferocities and subterfuges attending the competition for marriage partners are forgotten by the visitors to Norman Abbey. Yet here, in the depths of the country, the dominant emotion is boredom. Lord Henry Amundeville seems to be the only person purposefully and fully occupied. Day after day, with the same cold precision, he attends to government matters as a member of the Tory Privy Council, deals with poachers and wretched unmarried mothers in his capacity as a Justice of the Peace, finds time to interview lawyers, architects and picture dealers, interferes on behalf of his party in county elections for seats in the House of Commons, and as a landlord and gentleman farmer keeps an eye on his rents, his agricultural labourers, his blue-ribbon cattle and prize pigs. The narrator has a certain qualified respect for this man of impeccable industry and honour, despite his politics. At least he is not, like Wordsworth and Southey, a turncoat conservative. Lord Henry could never for a moment have entertained a liberal view on anything, not only because he is a Tory born and bred, but because he possesses no imagination whatever, and very little human feeling.

Like all his possessions, Lady Adeline is flawless. An acknowledged beauty whose chastity has never been impugned, a model wife and brilliant hostess, she has already produced the necessary male heir and is entirely devoted to the husband she married at eighteen. This at least is how she appears, after three years of marriage, to society, to Lord Henry and to herself. Far more intelligent, sophisticated and (on the surface) less emotional than Julia, Adeline is like Juan's first love in being both imaginative and (underneath her calm composure) passionate. With her, too, Juan will trigger off a belated and somewhat surprised recognition that her 'ideal' marriage is in fact loveless and dead. Yet there is no great disparity of ages here, as there was in Julia's case. Lord Henry's sexlessness is a product of temperament, not time. The consequences, however, of Lady Adeline's entanglement with her husband's young Spanish friend, as Byron hints darkly, will be even more explosive: she is 'the fair most fatal Juan ever met' (XIII. 12).

It is sometimes claimed that the Juan/Adeline relationship, at least up to the point at which the poem breaks off, is a repetition of the Julia affair in Canto I. That is true only in that Byron clearly does mean the reader to compare Adeline with Julia, even as he permits her rival Aurora to summon up memories of Haidée. These retrospective glances are part of the general thickening of weave characteristic of these last cantos. The similarities that emerge, however, only render more striking the fundamental difference of Juan's situation here from anything previous. Byron even found himself obliged, significantly, to falsify his own chronology: Juan *ought* to be, at most, seventeen to Adeline's twenty-one. England, however, seems to have aged him as incomprehensibly (although less drastically) as it did Hamlet. Juan does not suddenly become thirty, as Hamlet does, but he is said now to be Adeline's junior by only six weeks (XIV. 51), reducing almost to nothing that age gap, so prominent in his relations with Julia, Gulbeyaz and Catherine, which had established even Haidée as her lover's senior by one year. Aurora Raby, moreover, the other principal object of Juan's attention, is something quite novel in his experience: a prospective partner who, for all her withdrawn gravity, is, at sixteen, significantly younger than he.

Names, in the English cantos, almost invariably characterize their bearers. Although some real people, known to Byron either personally or by reputation, hover like shadows behind the guests enumerated at Norman Abbey, for the purposes of the poem their names tend to say about them virtually all that needs to be known: Dick Dubious the metaphysician, Sir Henry Silvercup the great race-winner, General Fireface, the Duke of Dash, or those aggressive fortune-hunters, 'the six Miss

Rawbolds – pretty dears!' (XIII. 85). The essence of the
sensual duchess of Fitz-Fulke is contained in the four-letter
word approximated after the hyphen. Amundeville ('worldly
city'), although both more complicated and less restrictive than
these other names, is nonetheless entirely appropriate for the
hosts at Norman Abbey: flag-ships of an unabashedly material-
istic society. There is more to Henry and Adeline than that, and
yet they can scarcely disclaim the overtones of their name.
The most puzzling appellation is Aurora Raby's. Associations
with dawn, freshness and youthful innocence shine out, ap-
propriately enough, from her Christian name. Her uncommon
surname, on the other hand, as Thomas Ashton was the first
to point out, is that of a notoriously unpleasant and profligate
baron with whom both Byron's wife's family and his own
sister's impossible husband were closely linked. Put together,
they constitute an uneasy oxymoron: suggesting that Aurora's
impact upon Juan's life, as Byron planned it, could not have
been simply redemptive.

Aurora has sometimes been seen, notably by Bernard Beatty,
as a symbol of the heavenly, as opposed to the Amundevilles'
worldly, city, associated with that forlorn but still potent image
of the Virgin which gazes down from the ruins of the abbey
church. Beautiful and wealthy, the last orphan remnant of a
noble Catholic family to whose unfashionable religion she
remains true, her spirituality does seem to ally her with Norman
Abbey itself rather than with her fellow guests. Among them
she sits aloof, a critical if pitying stranger. For Juan, the
narrator suggests, 'such a character – / High, yet resembling
not his lost Haidée' (XV. 58) represents an entirely new experience. Haidée, 'Nature's all', had been 'a flower'; Aurora,
equally lovely and sincere, but significantly less warm, is said
to be a 'gem' – something precious but unyielding. She is the
first woman Juan has met for whom love and holy matrimony
are inseparable; certainly no seductress, and patently impossible
to seduce, she fascinates him by her very indifference, her
high-minded contempt for his worldly éclat. She is attractive,
and yet her cool reticences are exactly the ones which had
fascinated Byron in Annabella Milbanke, at a time when most

of the beauties in London (married and un-married) were languishing at his feet. It is one of the many temporal subtleties of *Don Juan* that the narrator, re-living his own ill-fated courtship of Annabella, should pretend to share his hero's uncertainty as to whether Aurora's behaviour reflects 'her coldness or her self-possession' (XV. 57): 'Could it be pride? / Or modesty, or absence, or inanity?' (78). It seems more than likely that Juan, intrigued by Aurora, just as Byron was by Annabella, was going to marry her and only then — when it was too late — discover the answer.

Meanwhile, Adeline's jealousy of the 'infantine' (XV. 45) guest she dismisses, with tell-tale harshness, as 'that prim, silent, cold Aurora Raby' (49), signals the dangerous drift of her own affections. As Lord Henry's wife, Adeline has social duties to discharge — most onerous in the country when she is obliged (in order to woo votes for the Tory interest) to charm the local gentry who flock on its 'open days' to dine at Norman Abbey. She acts this part almost alarmingly well, thanks to her 'mobility', only the occasional sidelong glance 'of weariness or scorn' (XVI. 96–7) betraying to a close observer like Juan her underlying ennui. In a note to the passage, Byron defines 'mobility' as 'an excessive susceptibility of immediate impressions — at the same time without *losing* the past; and ... though sometimes apparently useful to the possessor, a most painful and unhappy attribute'. A word used by Thomas Moore in his life of Byron to describe his chameleon nature, and by the poet himself when talking to Lady Blessington, it suggests that Adeline resembles her creator in ways that go beyond a shared admiration for Pope. Bored, as Byron often was himself, by the very society in which she is so bewitchingly effective, Adeline has the added disadvantage of being a woman: without even her husband's masculine resources and 'serious' occupations on which to expend her energy and markedly greater intelligence. She indulges in match-making for Juan — selecting a series of prospective partners to all of whom she could comfortably condescend, while pointedly ruling out Aurora — for lack of anything better to do. Meanwhile, despite her efforts to prevent it, her plump, amoral friend the duchess of Fitz-Fulke (whose husband is cheerfully tolerant, as Lord Henry could never be, of his wife's infidelity) manages to seduce Juan and so (almost certainly) impel Adeline down the road to her own catastrophic adultery.

Although the narrator teases his readers with its pretended uncertainty, that adultery is clearly foreshadowed by the spectre of the Black Friar which so terrifies Juan on its first (and genuine) appearance. This vengeful spirit, still mourning the dispossession of the monks by the Amundeville family during the reign of Henry VIII, appears not only at both the bridals and the death-beds of the usurpers, but also 'when aught is to befall / That ancient line' (XVI. Song 4). Adeline and Henry saw it during their honeymoon. It walks again now in anticipation of the scandal and disgrace that will taint the Amundeville name after it has been dragged through the divorce courts, the predictable consequence of Adeline's fall. Meanwhile, 'her frolic Grace − Fitz-Fulke' (XVI. 123) takes advantage of the legend and of Juan's manifest abstraction and uneasiness after his nocturnal encounter to frighten him into her arms. On its second appearance to the hero, the 'ghost' is only a lustful duchess in monk's robes, playing a prank. The first manifestation was another matter. Significantly, both Juan and Fitz-Fulke, when they make their belated appearance at breakfast the next morning, are suffering from post-coital *tristesse* in a particularly acute form. Juan looks as though he had combated with more than one supernatural spirit:

> Being wan and worn, with eyes that hardly brooked
> The light, that through the Gothic windows shone:
> Her Grace, too, had a sort of air rebuked −
> Seemed pale and shivered, as if she had kept
> A vigil, or dreamt rather more than slept.

> (XVII. 14)

Some mysterious sacrilege, as both the guilty parties seem aware, has been involved in this love-making. And here, fourteen stanzas into Canto XVII, Byron abruptly abandoned *Don Juan*, took an affectionate but firm leave of Teresa Guiccioli, and set off to what he sensed from the beginning of the enterprise would be his death in Greece.

Chapter 4

The after-life of *Don Juan*

Byron and the 'atrocious reader'

The word *reader*, in either its singular or plural form, occurs far more often in *Don Juan* (as the concordance reveals) than in all Byron's other poems put together. Entirely absent from *Childe Harold*, the noun appears on only thirteen occasions elsewhere, as opposed to thirty-five here. Even *English Bards and Scotch Reviewers* employs it no more than twice. To certain named individuals – Southey, Wellington, or Francis Jeffrey of the *Edinburgh Review* – Byron from time to time speaks directly in *Don Juan*, using the poem to send them a kind of public verse letter that he knows they will hasten (whether with outrage or pleasure) to read. He is also conscious of communicating with a large circle of friends and acquaintances back in England, not to mention his sister and Lady Byron: people who could be counted on, however much they disapproved, to seize on the cantos as they appeared. The reader, however, who comes to concern him most as *Don Juan* proceeds, is not one of these. Variously characterized by the narrator as 'chaste', 'kind', 'gentle', 'too gentle', 'lively', 'atrocious' and 'grim', this altogether more shadowy, anonymous figure, at whose reactions he can only guess, gradually assumes – rather like his 'Muse', a lady also diversely described – the importance of a character in the poem.

In Canto XIII, the narrator addresses this personage directly:

> Oh, reader! If that thou canst read, – and know,
>   'Tis not enough to spell, or even to read,
> To constitute a reader; there must go
>   Virtues of which both you and I have need.
> Firstly, begin with the beginning – (though
>   That clause is hard); and secondly, proceed;
> Thirdly, commence not with the end – or, sinning
> In this sort, end at least with the beginning.

(73)

For all its lightness of touch, this is by no means simple foolery. Byron is insisting, first of all, upon something critics have refused to grant him until comparatively recently: a recognition that, despite its appearance of casual accretiveness, *Don Juan* needs to be experienced as an evolving whole. It is itself a type of 'mobility' in that the narrator's mercurial involvement with the emotions and events of the moment never allows him to lose touch with the poem's past, and this is also the way it should be read. Readers who (as so often) do not 'proceed' beyond the first two cantos, who only dip into this long poem here and there, or concentrate on the English cantos at the end and ignore the rest, can have no sense of its complexity and greatness.

Byron's injunctions in Canto XIII do not really seem directed at his contemporaries. For them, the poem became available over a period of years, in irregularly spaced instalments, according to his own rate of production and the efficiency of Murray and (subsequently) Hunt. The readers he predicates, on the other hand, will confront *Don Juan* as a whole, from its beginning through to that ending he did not live to write: effectively, they are readers of the future, not the present. Byron had always tended to be suspicious of poets who reserved their 'laurels for posterity' (Dedication, 9). It was one of the accusations he levelled against the 'Lakers', reminding them that 'The major part of such appellants go / To − God knows where − for no one else can know.' This distrust persists even in the later cantos of *Don Juan* ('Why, I'm Posterity, and so are you; / And whom do we remember? Not a hundred', XII. 19), but it co-exists now with its opposite: a wistful hope that he might be justified after all (as Milton was) in appealing to 'the Avenger, Time' (Dedication, 10). It was a hope born partly out of resentment of all the abuse showered upon his poem, the extent to which it had been misunderstood, and partly out of what by now had become a lonely but entrenched conviction of its worth.

Of one thing Byron seems to have been fairly certain: this more perceptive readership, if it ever came into being, could not be female. It is plain that even at the start of his poem

Byron had a predominantly male audience in mind, as he had not to anything like the same extent in *Childe Harold*. It is to other men of the world that he chiefly addresses himself, relying upon a measure of common masculine experience which the opposite sex might like to read about and consider, but which by definition it could not share. Women were not responsible for the hostile reviews the poem provoked during Byron's lifetime. On the other hand, they did almost unanimously find it distasteful, a response uniting personalities as diverse as Harriette Wilson, Lady Byron, Augusta Leigh, Caroline Lamb and Teresa Guiccioli. Lady Blessington made *Don Juan* a prohibited subject in her conversations with Byron. 'Women all over the world', Byron commented,

always retain their Free masonry – and as that consists in the illusion of the Sentiment – which constitutes their sole empire – ... all works which refer to the *comedy* of the passions – & laugh at Sentimentalism – of course are proscribed by the whole *Sect.* – I never knew a woman who did not admire Rousseau – and hate Gil Blas & de Grammont and the like – for the same reason. – And I never met with a woman English or foreign who did not do as much by D. J.   (BLJ VIII. 148)

He was wearily accustomed to receiving passionate epistles from women he had never met, but when in 1822 he received 'a love letter from *Pimlico* from a lady whom I never saw in my life – but who hath fallen in love with me for having written *Don Juan*!', it was natural for him to assume that she must be 'either mad or *nau*[ghty]' (BLJ X. 29).

It would be wrong to describe Charlotte Brontë, Elizabeth Barrett Browning and George Eliot as sentimentalists. On the other hand, none of them was very appreciative of the '*comedy* of the passions', or indeed could be said to possess much of a sense of humour generally. All three greatly disliked *Don Juan*, as indeed many feminists do today, although not necessarily for the reasons Byron suggested. Sweeping social and cultural changes have rendered the poem's outspokenness about sexual matters, its agnosticism and comically disabused treatment of marriage and fidelity acceptable in the second half of the twentieth century to female as well as male readers. Women who continue to resent *Don Juan* are likely to do so now because the narrator's attitude towards their sex, so often remarkable for its sympathy and perception, can at other times be mocking or even hostile. This kind of contradictoriness, however, is endemic in *Don Juan*, affecting virtually every topic Byron takes up, with the significant exceptions of political freedom and the prevalence of cant. He has, moreover, a way of making amends for his occasional misogynistic gibes – as when he accuses women of being inveterate liars, only in the next moment to establish lies as 'but / The truth in masquerade', equally necessary to 'historians, heroes, lawyers, priests' (XI. 36–7), men who merely manage a universal art with less grace and style. As for poets, they are 'liars' by profession (III. 87), continually presenting 'the truth in masquerade':

> Truth's fountains may be clear – her streams are muddy,
> And cut through such canals of contradiction,
> That she must often navigate o'er fiction.
>
> (XV. 88)

For Byron's contemporaries, one of the more offensive features of the poem was the way its bawdy innuendos continually decoyed readers into pulling off the mask themselves, uncovering their own hypocrisies. The narrator's mock indignation at being thought to 'hint allusions never *meant*' (X. 88), involves more than just the odd satiric dig at Lady Byron. It is far from being the case, as he was perfectly aware, that 'when I speak, I *don't hint*, but *speak out*'. He hints all the time, and in ways that cunningly turn the reader, whether amused or outraged, into an accomplice. The innuendos of *Don Juan* are quite different from its obscene puns (the celebrated 'fall for lack of moisture quite a dry-Bob', for instance, at the end of the Dedication), or those passages – sometimes quite extended – of *double entendres* where underlying sexual references operate beneath a superficially blameless surface. Any genuinely innocent reader, even in Byron's day, could well take 'dry-Bob' as referring simply to 'Bob' Southey, without needing to know that it also meant, in Regency slang, coitus without emission, even as he or she was not obliged to notice the joke about Juan owing his success in Russia to 'an old woman and his post' (X. 29). Although such passages are less witty, as well as more decent, if the puns go unrecognized, they are usually quite viable. This, however, is not true of the narrator's innuendos: those moments in the poem when he begins to say something, and then slyly draws back, often with the help of a dash or a disclaimer, tricking the reader into involuntarily rushing on to supply the reprehensible word or thought.

Significantly, innuendos of this kind are almost entirely absent from the Haidée episode. The one exception, and it is isolated from the lovers themselves, occurs in connection with Lambro's homecoming. The modern voyager, less fortunate than Ulysses, may find on his return that his dog Argus 'bites him by − the breeches' (III. 23), the dash here (as at II. 7 and V. 139) directing attention towards the male private parts. Elsewhere, the narrator impels his reader to concur that lovers' quarrels are less likely to be made up over dinner than in bed ('And then − and then − and then − sit down and sup', I. 179), and that boys' schools are places of complex sexual initiation (I. 53). He traps them into imagining what the 'several other things, which I forget' might be for which the adolescent Juan yearns (I. 96), or into identifying the unmentionable item that Alfonso and his search-party find under Julia's bed (I. 144). Occasionally he adds insult to injury by pretending to rebuke readers for entertaining some 'unworthy' idea towards which in fact they have cunningly been propelled: 'the Moon' as an allusion to the menstrual cycle in Canto X (10−11), or the 'one vent' which nuns are said to find, in an Italian convent, for their passions: 'And what is that? Devotion, doubtless − how / Could you ask such a question?', VI. 32−3).

Byron enjoys teasing the reader, but his innuendos, like most of the jokes in the poem, have a serious purpose. They form part of his war on hypocrisy and cant, demonstrating how false the innocence of his 'chaste reader' really is. Even his friends were rendered jumpy and suspicious by them, frequently locating indecencies in the poem where in fact they did not exist. Byron was exasperated at having to point out to Hobhouse and the rest that the pail of 'housemaid's water' emptied over the narrator's head by young Juan in Canto I should not be supposed to contain urine. He may have been capable, in an outrageous and brilliant couplet which his friends forced him to excise in proof, of a description of Donna Inez's Sunday school for naughty boys, where 'Their manners mending, and their morals curing, / She taught them to suppress their vice and urine.' In pointless indecency, of the kind foisted on him with regard to the 'housemaid's water', he had no interest at all. It was the innumerable imitators of *Don Juan* – including some who claimed to be attacking the lewdness and irreligion of the original – who purveyed that.

English imitations, forgeries and continuations

Byron's literary and personal celebrity had for years tempted various lesser writers to publish their own works, usually highly derivative, under his name. The consequences could be embarrassing – as when Byron's physician, the hopeless Polidori, fathered *The Vampyre* on his former employer, a tale concocted from the one Byron had planned during the ghost-story session at Diodati that produced Mary Shelley's *Frankenstein*. Goethe promptly mistook it for the consummate expression of Byron's genius. 'It is enough to answer for what I have written', Byron once complained, 'but it were too much for Job himself to bear what one has not – I suspect that when the Arab Patriarch wished that "his Enemy had written a book", he did not anticipate his own name on the title page' (BLJ V.85). In the case of *Don Juan*, spurious 'continuations' in English began to appear as early as 1819, between the publication of the first two cantos and that of Cantos III, IV and V. They persisted for the remainder of Byron's life and, after his death, turned into a flood as attempts were made throughout the nineteenth century either to finish or merely to imitate the poem, sometimes by authors pretending to have discovered new cantos among Medwin's or the Countess Guiccioli's papers, or even (in one case) to have taken them down by dictation from Byron's ghost.

Only two of these works possess any value in themselves. The anonymous *Don Leon*, a poem in couplets, written during the 1830s but not printed until 1866, purports to be Byron's account of his own bisexuality. Digressive and often obscene, it incorporates — along with a tormented inconsistency in its attitude to homoeroticism reminiscent of the contradictions of *Don Juan* itself — what is clearly a serious plea for reform of the law which still made homosexual acts punishable in England by death. In 1841, during his incarceration in the asylum at High Beech, Epping, John Clare produced the deranged but savagely powerful 'Don Juan A Poem', an *ottava rima* attack on what he saw as the perverted sexuality of London society, written by a poet sometimes aware that Byron is someone else, and dead, and sometimes persuaded that he is Clare himself, 'still in Allens madhouse caged & living'. Apart from these two highly individual works, the nineteenth-century imitations and continuations are of interest chiefly because they help to isolate and define the qualities of Byron's masterpiece, what only its author could have written.

Predictably, a number of these parasitic efforts either reform Juan (and sometimes his creator) or self-righteously send one or both to Hell, reaching back by way of Byron to Tirso da Molina's essentially moralistic and Christian fable. Some parody, while others openly attack, the poem. In most of those that condescend to have a story, Juan again becomes the aggressor, a heartless seducer of wronged and helpless women, while the sentimentality Byron had mocked creeps back, not infrequently combined with a smuttiness, a kind of lubricity foreign to the original. George Reynolds' *A Sequel to Don Juan* (1843) elaborates upon Juan's deflowering of the governess Rosa in detail so salacious as to make Byron's reference to 'those deep and burning moments' (II. 195) of Juan and Haidée's love-making seem a model of reticence and delicacy:

> Yes — when, no longer coy, she sinks in pleasure
>   Upon your bosom, — when her virgin charms
> Surrender, amid sighs, their choicest treasure, —
>   When new emotions triumph o'er alarms,
> And teach her ecstasies beyond all measure; —

> When, palpitating – blushing, in your arms
> Her flashing eyes and panting lips apart
> Proclaim

> (III. 30)

et cetera, et cetera. What Byron would have thought of this repellent male fantasy – especially in conjunction with the author's subsequent heavy-handed moralizing over 'virtue sacrificed and rifled charms' (III. 31) – is not difficult to imagine. Again, in G. R. Wythen Baxter's *Don Juan Junior* (1839), descriptions of the 'dove-some eyes ... of deep sea-blue' (I. 14) of the violated maiden who, clasping her seducer's knees, 'with many a tear – her boon's presage, / Entreatingly murmured – "*Marriage!*"' (32) co-exist with leers at a young commandant caught 'in a certain position with his bride, / Which none but the newspapers can describe' (70).

'Dove-some' is a 'poetic' epithet inconceivable in *Don Juan* itself. (Even 'dove', as a rhyme word, was pilloried by Byron as 'that good old steam-boat which keeps verses moving', IX. 74.) Adjectives in his poem generally have the forceful and inspired simplicity of fact:

> There the large olive rains its amber store
>   In marble fonts; there grain, and flower, and fruit,
> Gush from the earth until the land runs o'er;
>   But there too many a poison-tree has root,
> And midnight listens to the lion's roar,
>   And long, long deserts scorch the camel's foot.

> (IV. 55)

Byron initially tried out 'boundless' as the adjective modifying his African 'deserts'. Then he replaced it in the manuscript with the purposefully reiterated 'long', seeing that his first choice was literary and false, his second – like 'large', and 'marble' both truthful and emotionally accurate. The noun 'store', so familiar in the work of eighteenth-century nature poets like Thomson, is transformed (indeed liquified) by the precision of 'amber'. There may be nothing in *Don Juan* to compete with the unexpected, revelatory force of an adjective such as 'clammy' in Keats' description, in the 'Ode to Autumn', of the 'cells' of a honeycomb at summer's end;

Byron's more straightforward evocation of 'cooks in motion with their clean arms bared' (V.50) is, in its different way, equally distinctive, and quite beyond the capacities of his imitators.

Although many of them tried to copy his use of innuendo, the results are usually without purpose. In the anonymous 'A Touch at an Unpublished Canto of Don Juan' (*The Newcastle Magazine*, 1, 1822), for instance, Juan, fleeing from the wrath of Lambro, descries in a distant bay:

> A ship — which he to help him off beseeched,
> Making the signal with — in fact, he stood unbreeched.
>
> They were the very — breeches Haidée made
>   And gave him, when she found him on the shore
> Without a pair of drawers, as I have said.

The reader is expected to snigger, simply for sniggering's sake, at the sight of a trouserless man. Apart from its limp half-rhyme, 'as I have said' is mere conversational padding, the kind of feeble apeing of Byron's manner that frequently makes it difficult to establish the nature of these imitations: pastiche, parody, or simple incompetence?

Nudity, in a number of them, figures as a source of titillation shiftily combined with moral outrage. The unknown author of *The Seventeenth Canto of Don Juan* (1829) is not un-typical in the way he giggles at the marble gods and cupids with which he has populated Lord Henry's garden walks — 'not obligated or to leaf or feather, / To keep their tender members from the air' (133) — while at the same time fulminating against this shameless display: one which 'must raise unhallowed sentiments' (128) in female breasts. The writer's affected prudery sometimes seems worthy of Donna Inez herself: as when he complains that maidens curious to discover from the statuary whether gentlemen's ' "inexpressibles" ' are 'wide/Or narrow there, or just as they are worn/At morning promenade or evening ball' (139), are likely to find that '*oh diable!* they have none at all!' The painstaking reproduction here both of Byron's characteristic scattering of foreign words and his glancing Shakespearean allusions — one advancing cupid is said to cause prurient dreams by showing 'the very front of his offending' — debase their model.

By no means all the authors of poems parasitic on *Don Juan* used *ottava rima*. Those who did usually found themselves locked in a struggle with the form that throws Byron's accomplished ease into vivid relief. Even W. H. Auden, that master of verse technique, was later to apologize in his 'Letter to Lord Byron' (1936) for avoiding it:

> *Ottava rima* would, I know, be proper,
> The proper instrument on which to pay
> My compliments, but I should come a cropper;
> Rhyme-royal's difficult enough to play.

Auden was more honest than the author of *Don Juan Junior*, who attempted in his preface to forestall accusations of technical incompetence by announcing that he had deliberately 'availed himself of the most extreme metrical license', considering the rules and 'systematic jingle' of his chosen form 'too exactive, and apt, by their Draconian severity, to cramp and confine a poet's expression of his thoughts'.

Again and again, in their search for comic rhymes (especially to conclude a stanza), the nineteenth-century imitators fell back on Byron's own. 'Nunnery/gunnery', 'adultery/sultry', even the pairing of 'Juan' with Ossian's 'Duan', are among the many shamelessly repeated by poets who, unable to play Byron's exhilarating games with the English language, did not scruple to annex his *trouvailles*. When they do launch out on their own, the results are usually either banal or grotesque. Byron's 'there are months which nature grows more merry in, / March has its hares, and May must have its heroine' (I. 102) is brilliant; its imitation — 'This vision, gentle reader, know of me, / Is meant for this Canto's Heroiné' (I. 12) — is merely limping. The same is true of all those laboured emulations of the *Don Juan* narrator rummaging in public for a simile or a rhyme:

> Within this lake a little island lay,
>   Verdant and smiling, like — I know not what;
> Having no simile, I therefore pray

> The reader just to picture such a spot
> Upon his mental tablet, if a ray
> Of sentiment is in him ...

> But stay, I've got a metaphor, I think, —
> Not one, I'm sure, that all will comprehend;
> At least not those who never chanced to drink
> Good whiskey punch.
>
> (*The Seventeenth Canto of Don Juan*, 122–3)

Byron's impatient rejection of that 'tired metaphor' the snow-capped volcano as a description of Adeline — 'I'll have another figure in a trice: — / What say you to a bottle of champagne? / Frozen into a very vinous ice' (XIII. 36–7) — is justly famous. His 1829 imitator in *The Seventeenth Canto of Don Juan* only succeeds in putting his impoverished and derivative imagination embarrassingly on view.

The real trouble with most of these pseudo *Don Juans*, apart from their emotional and moral dishonesty and their failures of technique, is that their authors have little or nothing to say but try instead to mimic the voice of a complex narrator with so much on his mind that he never gets round to expressing half of it. They trivialize Byron, reducing the powerful, unpredictable play of his intelligence, his kaleidoscopic moods and personality, to something narrow and mechanical. When they digress, it is not because their minds have spontaneously leaped from one idea to another, because they are suddenly angry, nostalgic, elated, despondent or bemused, or want for some particular purpose to hold up the story, but merely because this is what Byron did. Like Cleopatra's Antony, the narrator of *Don Juan* is a dolphin, effortlessly sporting through the element — *ottava rima* — in which he lives. His English imitators often seem to be trying hard not to drown. At their best (and this is true even of Auden, amusing though 'A Letter to Lord Byron' is), they merely chatter.

Don Juan and the spirit of revolution

In his account of nineteenth-century English and American sequels or imitations of Byron's poem, S.C. Chew states categorically that their number is 'without parallel, it is safe to say, in the history of literature'. Chew's list includes novels as well as poems, and also dramatic works such as John Baldwin Buckstone's engagingly titled *A New Don Juan! An Operatical, Poetical, Egotistical, Melodramatical, Extravaganzical, but Strictly Moral Burletta, in Two Acts; Founded on Lord Byron's Celebrated Poem*, performed at the Adelphi Theatre, London in 1828. Carefully researched, but by no means complete, Chew's bibliography immediately provokes a question: why should *Don Juan*, the object of such obloquy, nonetheless have received these widespread and extraordinary attentions? Byron's celebrity, coupled with the desire to parody or savage his poem in its own mode, can account for the phenomenon only in part. It is true that most of the reviews of Cantos I and II mingled censure with grudging admiration of the work's brilliance. Later cantos, on the other hand, especially IX onwards, were reviewed more perfunctorily in those upper-middle-class journals which represented the literary establishment (this response probably owed something to the rapidity with which these instalments appeared), and with dismissals or denigrations of their artistic achievement as well as their morals. The noble author (they tended to lament) had entered a period of sad decline.

Byron himself was well aware of his diminished popularity not only with the critics, but also among those well-heeled members of the public who had once besieged the book-shops, and Murray's elegant premises in Albemarle Street, for copies of his eastern tales. 'And yet I can't help scribbling once a week', he observed ruefully in Canto XIV, 'Tiring old readers, nor discovering new' (10). He was right about the old readers, but wrong about the new. *Don Juan* had, in fact, already acquired an audience socially different from the one which had abandoned him and far greater in size. Byron nagged Murray in vain to bring out the poem in a cheap edition as well as in expensive quarto or octavo volumes, the formats associated with his earlier work, but impossible for the literate working and lower-middle classes to afford. Murray had asked thirty-one shillings and sixpence for Cantos I and II. John Hunt issued Cantos VI, VII and VIII for only a shilling. Byron and Hunt, moreover, proved unable to prevent cheap, pirated editions of the poem from flooding onto the market. On 8 August 1822, in a case subsequently reported in *The Examiner*, one of these rogue publishers, William Dugdale, actually pleaded in the Vice-chancellor's Court for the removal of the injunction granted against him for infringement of copyright, on the grounds that *Don Juan* was, in fact, a work too licentious and immoral for the law to protect. Full, he declared, of scenes 'calculated to produce the worst effect on the mind of those inexperienced persons who might read them, and destructive of the moral feeling of the community', this book ridiculing Church, State and 'everything that dignified human nature', was one that no 'father of a family' could possibly introduce into his home. The market Dugdale himself aimed at was, by implication, of the lowest social as well as moral kind.

The consequences of making Byron's poem available in inexpensive, popular editions proved to be considerable. When, in 1990, William St Clair published his revelatory statistical analysis of the nineteenth-century print-runs of *Don Juan*, not only as marketed officially by Murray and Hunt but also by a number of clandestine London publishers like Dugdale (and about twenty of these were operating in the first ten years alone), it became clear both that Friedrich Engels was more accurate than has commonly been supposed when he maintained, in 1844, that it was the workers, not the hypocritical bourgeoisie, who really knew and cherished Byron's work, and that *Don Juan*, above all, was the poem they had taken to heart. Byron seems a little tentative in Canto VIII when he turns to address directly the 'Cockneys of London!' (124), urging them to resist military conscription and the inequities of the ruling powers. It was not the audience he knew. Yet his poem reached both the urban and the rural poor. Even without trying to establish the number of readers who might share a single cheap copy, St Clair concludes from the number printed and sold that 'within a decade, *Don Juan* had penetrated far deeper into the reading of the nation than any other modern book, with the possible exception of Tom Paine's *Rights of Man*, and new pirate editions were still being put on the market in the 1830s'. It was read, he concludes, 'by many thousands who did not read any of Byron's other works, and it was probably read by thousands who read no other book of any kind except the Bible'.

The news of Byron's death in the Greek War of Independence briefly shocked many people in England, but it made him a hero to the rebellious poor. When the poet's funeral procession passed through London on the way to Nottingham and interment in the family vault – burial in Westminster Abbey having been refused him – the aristocracy sent a long line of empty carriages to attend it, and stayed at home themselves. The streets, on the other hand, were lined with people. When the cortège reached Nottingham itself, a local observer remarked with disgust that his lordship had been 'a lover of liberty, which the Radical Corporation here thought made him their brother; therefore all the rabble rout from every lane and alley, and garret and cellar, came forth to ... shout and push, in his honour'. It was *Don Juan*, however, which kept Byron's memory fresh and made his portrait such a familiar presence in Chartist homes.

On 27 June 1838, in one of the earliest and largest of the Chartist demonstrations, at Newcastle, many of the banners flaunted quotations from the poem. In 1847, at a time when Byron's reputation was sinking among the middle and upper classes to a low from which it would not really begin to recover until the end of the century, at a time when Carlyle and Thackeray, Tennyson, Newman, Macaulay, Ruskin, Browning and Swinburne either had repudiated, or were about to repudiate, his work, *The Northern Star*, a radical paper, asserted boldly that *Don Juan* was 'a record of free thought and an eloquent vindication of democracy, which every republican, every lover of his species, should have in his library'. Not many of the tenements and cottages of the poor rose to a 'library', but a well-thumbed copy of *Don Juan* (to the dismay of the clergy) could be found in a surprising number of them.

Chartist poets, as Philip Collins has observed, did not try to imitate *Don Juan*. The poem's influence within the movement was ideological, not literary: as a rallying-point for political and social reform, and also for the freedom of individual speech, thought and personal behaviour. The effect, of course, was to render it still more opprobrious among conservative defenders of the status quo. Even John Morley, who in 1870 contributed a lengthy and sympathetic piece on Byron to the *Fortnightly Review* in which he contrasted Byron's towering stature outside England with the slight regard of his own country, and identified his voice as that of European Revolution incarnate, firmly condemned *Don Juan*. Its very wit and power had made 'an anti-social and licentious sentiment attractive to puny creatures, who were thankful to have their lasciviousness so gaily adorned'. The British may, he wrote, have 'deserved *Don Juan*', in that their lack of respect for aspirations and ideas not sanctified by religious platitude merited chastisement. The poem seemed to him, nonetheless, to embody the worst aspect of the revolutionary spirit: it made 'the passions of the individual his own law', and (in particular) it was guilty of denigrating marriage and the sanctities of family life.

Morley did not overestimate the impact upon nineteenth-century Europe of Byron's personality, life and work. For at least two decades after his death, 'Byronism' continued to be a potent force on the continent, in both literary and political terms. It is by no means easy to single out the response to *Don Juan* in particular, and certainly true that the satiric Byron had less influence upon European Romanticism than the poet of *Childe Harold*, *Manfred*, the lyric poems and eastern tales. *Don Juan* was, on the whole, slower to be translated and initially more limited in its appeal. Yet a significant number of writers did latch onto Byron's epic and, in a number of cases, allowed their own work to be influenced by it.

In France, most readers were initially shocked by Cantos I and II − not so much on moral grounds as because the image they cherished, that of a tormented, melancholy fatalist, was rudely shattered by the poem's gaiety and irreverence. Mérimée and also Stendhal, who had disliked Byron when he met him but admired *Don Juan* from the start, were exceptions. Then, in the 1830s, a few dissenting spirits – the young Hugo, Lamartine, Vigny – began to pay serious attention to this last, unfinished work. Some of the early writing of Gautier bears its impress and, it has been argued, de Musset derived from it a new narrative technique. Apart from Vigny, most of these writers were dependent upon Amédée Pichot's sorry French translation. (Byron himself, in 1821, had seen and not been impressed by his version of Cantos I–V.) In Russia – where the poet Ryleyev, one of the leaders of the Decembrist rising of 1825, carried a volume of Byron with him as he went to his execution – Lermontov and Pushkin were also forced to rely upon Pichot. Yet in Russia too, even in this less than satisfactory form, *Don Juan* made its presence felt.

Two long poems by Lermontov, *Saška* (1885–6) and *Children's Fairytale* (1840), owe something to it, as to some extent does his novel, *A Hero of Our Time* (1839–41). In a letter of 4 November 1823, Pushkin explicitly compared his *Evgeny Onegin* to *Don Juan*. A number of specific resemblances can be identified: the digressions and easy conversational tone of *Evgeny Onegin*, an impression of ceaseless and brilliant improvisation, the balance of parody with feeling, and a profound concern with time and change. Pushkin, however, conceived of *Evgeny Onegin* as 'a novel in verse', not an epic satire. Not only is the fourteen-line stanza he employed very different from Byron's *ottava rima*, but the range and scope of the poem are consciously much smaller, the story it has to tell far more closely allied to novels of sentiment than to the picaresque. Considerably later, in his story 'The Black Monk', Chekhov was to resurrect the spectral black friar whose appearance so alarmed Juan at Norman Abbey.

Like the Countess Guiccioli, most Italians were also dependent upon Pichot for their knowledge of *Don Juan*, with the added complication that even after Byron's death his works were suppressed in Italy by the authorities, and had to be clandestinely obtained. Although in 1825 an anonymous elegy ('Stanze alla memoria di Lord Byron') used *ottava rima* to celebrate the poet who had given his life for Greece, an Italian translation of *Don Juan* in that verse form had to wait until 1865. Long before then, Byron's name had become a talisman among republicans striving for a free and united Italy, who mourned his death (as Mazzini wrote eloquently in 1839) as if for the noblest of her own sons.

In nineteenth-century Germany, where Goethe immediately pronounced Cantos I and II 'a work of boundless genius', the reputation of the poem from the start ran high. Goethe himself, although for long a devoted admirer of Byron, seems to have been secretly troubled by *Don Juan* – perhaps, as E. M. Butler has suggested, because in it he was confronted for the first time with the full force of the English writer's personality: not simply its fatalism and melancholy, but the concomitant gaiety and outrageous wit. He began a translation but abandoned it, partly because he recognized that Germany at the time had no cultured comic language, but also, almost certainly, because while at some moments he staunchly defended the original from charges of indecency, at others he suspected it might be 'the most immoral work poetic art has ever produced'. His own fragmentary effort, which he deposited in the library at Weimar, was to be borrowed only by personal friends. Less august translators, however, were almost immediately in action. A complete *Don Juan* in German became available in 1830, and other translations were issued and reprinted throughout the century. Even before that, Christian Grabbe, whose English was excellent, had purchased a complete *Don Juan* and, in 1830, produced a tragedy – *Don Juan und Faust* – in which he married the Don Juan story to its persistent twin, that myth of Faust which Byron had already explored in *Manfred* and which (as Grabbe recognized) he had felt impelled in 1822 to resurrect and run alongside *Don Juan* in *The Deformed Transformed*, his last, brilliant (and similarly unfinished) verse play. In contrast to France, where interest in Byron declined after 1850, Germany continued to regard him as a hero of the struggle for social, political and aesthetic freedom, and (prophetically) to hold *Don Juan* in particular esteem.

To trace the artistic influence of the poem across the rest of Europe would be a formidable task, well beyond the scope of this book. Ibsen in the fourth act of *Peer Gynt*, the Spanish poet Espronceda in *Estudiante de Salamanca* and *El Diablo mundo*, Poland's Adam Mickiewicz and Juliusz Słovacki, are a few writers among many who drew from Byron's poem. In 1883, the Polish translator of *Don Juan* actually used Słovacki's digressive verse tale *Beniowski*, written (in *ottava rima*) some forty years earlier, as a model for his own rendering of Byron's original. Byron's poem was apparently a formative influence upon the Hungarian verse novel. In striking contrast to England, where *Don Juan* spawned only feeble and parasitic imitations, on the continent it became a liberating and enabling model: helping very different writers, operating in a number of languages, to discover their own, individual voices and forms.

Distance, both cultural and geographical, and a different language, seem on the whole to be prerequisites for any genuinely creative use of Byron's poem. Certainly England, unlike the continent, has remained signally unable to produce anything but parody or pastiche. In the nineteenth century, this was true not only of the multitude of poetasters who perpetrated imitations or forgeries, but even of Keats, whose late unfinished work *The Cap and Bells* (1819), an essay in the manner (although not the stanzaic form) of *Don Juan*, manages only to seem uncharacteristic and trivial. Anthony Trollope constitutes a rare exception. The eponymous hero of his political novels *Phineas Finn* (1869) and *Phineas Redux* (1876) has been persuasively identified by Robert Polhemus, partly on the basis of references by Trollope himself, as a direct descendant of Byron's hero, possessed of the 'passive, subtle and erotic charm and sensibility of Juan', and like him the occasion not only for social observation and assessment, but also the civilizing of Eros.

In the twentieth century, at least one European poet of stature allowed *Don Juan* to preside compellingly over poems wrested out of extreme political hardship and suffering. When Isaiah Berlin visited Anna Akhmatova in Leningrad in 1945, she told him that before reading some of her own work she wished to recite 'two cantos [*sic*] of Byron's *Don Juan* ... for they were relevant to what would follow'. According to Berlin, who was unable to identify or even understand the passages (presumably she meant two *stanzas*) because of her impenetrable Russian pronunciation of English, she spoke the lines from memory, eyes closed, and with intense emotion. It seems possible, however, given the use of Byron's 'In my hot youth – when George the Third was King' (I.212) as an epigraph for Part I of her 'Poem Without A Hero' – one of the works she subsequently read to Berlin – that Akhmatova may have identified her own sense of a haunting and irrecoverable past era with Byron's lament at the end of Canto I of *Don Juan* (212–17) for a society, now vanished, that included a passionate younger self.

Akhmatova's use of Byron (she remembers him, in the same poem, as a symbol of Romanticism, lighting Shelley's funeral pyre while 'All the world's skylarks shattered / The dome beneath eternity') belongs in the great European tradition. Twentieth-century English poets, by contrast, have remained content simply to imitate the manner of *Don Juan* – not only Auden in his 'Letter to Lord Byron', but (among others) George Barker in *The True Confession of George Barker* (1950–64), A.D. Hope in his *ottava rima* 'A Letter from Rome' (1958), and Edwin Morgan in 'Byron at Sixty-Five' (1987). These poems are often witty and attractive, but their art is essentially that of the ventriloquist, their rationale oddly akin to the one which continues to impel novelists to reconstruct Byron's lost 'Memoirs' (Robert Nye, 1990), fantasize about his life and erotic entanglements (Sigrid Combüchen, *Byron: A Novel*, 1990), or even, as in Amanda Prantera's *Conversations with Lord Byron on Perversion, 163 Years after His Lordship's Death* (1987), invent a computer which, fed every available piece of information about the poet's life, work and correspondence, begins to function as Byron's voice from beyond the grave. Writers continue to be strangely obsessed by this man, often to the extent of wanting to get into Byron's skin themselves, to speak with his voice. If they are poets, *Don Juan* is the work to which they usually turn, not simply because it is Byron's masterpiece, but because there the personality by which they are fascinated is most fully present.

Epilogue

The response to *Don Juan* in nineteenth-century America (apart from a certain amount of approving interest in what Byron had to say about George Washington and Daniel Boone) was similar to that in England. Although untroubled by the poem's anti-monarchical sentiments or its incitements to revolution and social reform, Americans immediately concurred about its irreligion and indecency. Just as in England, however, all the obloquy showered upon it in the New World did not prevent a host of minor poets from trying their hand at imitations. Fitz-Greene Halleck's *Fanny*, 'a pseudo Don Juan / With the wickedness out that gave salt to the true one', as James Russell Lowell put it, appeared in 1819. It was succeeded by many others, all – with one exception, *Susie Knight* (1863), the only known copy of which was still kept in a locked drawer at the beginning of this century – of impeccable moral purity: John Brainard's 'New Year's Verses for 1825', William Simms' *Donna Florida* (1843), Nathaniel Willis' *Lady Jane* (1844), or George Lunt's *Julia*, five cantos of *ottava rima* published in 1855.

There were also a number of attempts to finish or continue Byron's poem, including one dramatization: *The Sultana, or A Trip to Turkey* (1822), in which Haidée follows Juan to Constantinople in male attire. These, on the whole, are neither better nor worse than their British equivalents. The major American writers – all but one – ignored *Don Juan*. Although Edgar Allan Poe was much obsessed with Byron, this particular poem (predictably) was not one that attracted him. Newstead Abbey may well, as Katrina Bachinger has argued, be the model for Poe's sombre and ruinous Gothic pile, the house of Usher, but the connection seems to have been made by way of Washington Irving's description of the place rather than by Cantos XIII–XVII of *Don Juan*. The one exception is Herman Melville, whose personal copy of Byron's poem survives. It is not only annotated ('Byron is a better man in *Don Juan* than in his serious poems' he scribbled approvingly at one point), but also heavily underlined. The anti-war passages, and many of those dealing with social hypocrisy, human cruelty and the predicament of the artist, had (as might be expected) a special appeal for the author of *Moby-Dick* and *Pierre*. Otherwise, the important figures in American Romanticism, unlike their European counterparts, seem to have remained untouched by Byron's greatest poem.

America, however, has made handsome amends for its original neglect. When, in the early twentieth century, Byron's reputation began to recover from its late nineteenth-century eclipse, it became apparent that *Don Juan* was gradually establishing itself as its author's finest and most important work. As the century has progressed, more and more of the canon – including the once-despised plays, individual poems such as 'Darkness' or the stanzas 'To the Po', even the eastern tales – has been rehabilitated, but without any serious questioning of the pre-eminence of Byron's masterpiece in *ottava rima*. Changes in taste, and also in critical ideas about how certain kinds of poem can and should be read, have benefited Byron, restoring him as a major writer. *Don Juan* no longer seems 'impure' either morally or in aesthetic terms. That this should now be recognized so widely owes much to the work of a group of dedicated and brilliant American scholars: Leslie Marchand, Willis Pratt, T. G. Steffan, Ernest J. Lovell, Jr. and Jerome McGann.

Marchand's three-volume biography of Byron appeared in 1957 and immediately superseded all other accounts. Here at last was a comprehensive, thoroughly documented life, incorporating a wealth of new material, which revealed (without special pleading) a Byron both compelling and sympathetic. Marchand then addressed himself to the task of editing the complete letters and journals, assembling in an eleven-volume edition a mass of previously unpublished material, while restoring to their original form texts bowdlerized by Prothero in his six-volume edition (1891–1901). Marchand's edition was completed in 1982. Both the biography and the edition were of incalculable service to *Don Juan*, as well as to Byron more generally. They associated the poem firmly with its author's life and times, encouraging – as the New Criticism receded, and with it the notion of the autonomous, contextless work of art – the kind of reading to which it was by nature most fully responsive.

The need for a new, fully annotated edition of the poem itself was met in 1957, the year Marchand published his biography, by the so-called 'Variorum', produced in four volumes by Steffan and Pratt. Here, for the first time, Byron's manuscripts were examined and analysed, and the amount of work and revision that had gone into the finished poem revealed. The edition presented *Don Juan* as Byron had wanted it: as a serious, consequential satire of lasting importance and greatness. The detailed account of the stages of its creation ('The Anvil of Composition') in volume I has proved especially valuable. In 1973, again as Byron would have wished, Steffan and Pratt made a (not entirely satisfactory) text and a judicious selection of the Variorum notes available in a popular (Penguin) edition. In 1986 Jerome McGann published what has become the authoritative text of *Don Juan* as volume V of the new Clarendon Press edition of Byron's complete poetical works: a monumental undertaking, whose consequences for Byron scholarship and the poet's reputation have still to be fully grasped. (This text is also reproduced in full in McGann's selected Byron for the Oxford Authors series.) McGann himself, meanwhile, in a series of major books and articles, put forward new ways of reading *Don Juan*, within both a classical and a European political context, that for many readers transformed the poem.

Francis Bacon, a writer Byron admired, once ventured the opinion that critics were 'the brushers of noblemen's clothes'. *Don Juan*, after a period of rather shabby neglect, now confronts the twenty-first century in resplendent attire: the wit and brilliance of this 'versified Aurora Borealis, / Which flashes o'er a waste and icy clime' (VII.2), able to communicate at last with the audience for which, over one hundred and fifty years after Byron's death, it sometimes seems to have been written.

Guide to further reading

Works mentioned in the text

Akhmatova, Anna, 'Poem Without A Hero', in *You Will Hear Thunder. Akhmatova: Poems*, trans. D.M. Thomas (London, 1985).

Ashton, Thomas, 'Naming Byron's Aurora Raby', *English Language Notes*, 7 (December 1969), 114–20.

Bachinger, Katrina, 'An Autumn at Newstead: A Source for "The Fall of the House of Usher" ', *Byron Journal*, 13 (1985), 4–21.

Beatty, Bernard, *Byron's Don Juan* (Totowa, New Jersey, 1985).

Berlin, Isaiah, *Personal Impressions* (London, 1980).

Blessington, Marguerite, countess of, *Conversations of Lord Byron*, ed. Ernest J. Lovell, Jr. (Princeton, 1969).

Butler, E.M., *Byron and Goethe* (London, 1956).

Chew, S.C., *Byron in England: His Fame and After Fame* (London, 1924).

Clare, John, 'Don Juan', in *The Later Poems of John Clare 1837–64*, I, ed. Eric Robinson and David Powell (Oxford, 1984).

Collins, Philip, 'Thomas Cooper, the Chartist: Byron and the "Poets of the Poor" ' (Nottingham Byron Lecture, 1969).

Davie, Donald, *Purity of Diction in English Verse* (London, 1952).

De Almeida, Hermione, *Byron and Joyce Through Homer: Don Juan and Ulysses* (London, 1981).

Eliot, T.S., 'Byron' (1937), rpt. in *On Poets and Poetry* (New York, 1957).

Frere, John Hookham, *The Monks and the Giants* (1817), ed. A.D. Waller (London, 1926).

Gardner, Dame Helen, '*Don Juan*' (1958), rpt. in *Byron: A Collection of Critical Essays*, ed. P. West (Twentieth Century Views series, Englewood, New Jersey, 1963).

Graham, Peter, *Don Juan and Regency England* (London, 1990).

Hazlitt, William, 'Conversations of John Northcote, Esq. R.A.' (1830), in *The Complete Works of William Hazlitt*, ed. P.P. Howe, 21 vols. (London), XI, pp. 279–80.

Huxley, Aldous, 'Tragedy and the Whole Truth', in *Music at Night* (London, 1931).

Knight, G. Wilson, *Byron: Christian Virtues* (London, 1952).

Lockhart, John G., *John Bull's Letter to Lord Byron*, ed. A.L. Strout (Oklahoma, 1947).

Medwin, Thomas, *Medwin's Conversations with Lord Byron*, ed.
    Ernest J. Lovell, Jr. (Princeton, 1966).
Morley, John, 'Byron' (1871), rpt. in *Byron: The Critical Heritage*,
    ed. A. Rutherford (London, 1970), pp. 384–409.
Polhemus, Robert, 'Being In Love in *Phineas Finn/Phineas Redux*:
    Desire, Devotion, Consolation', in *Nineteenth Century Fiction*,
    37 (3), December 1982.
Severn, Joseph Andrew, quoted in Walter Jackson Bate, *John Keats*
    (London, 1963).
The Complete Works of Percy Bysshe Shelley, ed. Thomas Hutchinson
    (Oxford, 1934).
St Clair, William, 'The Impact of Byron's Writings', in *Byron:
    Augustan and Romantic*, ed. A. Rutherford (London, 1990).
Wilson, Harriette, quoted in George Paston and Peter Quennell,
    *'To Lord Byron': Feminine Profiles Based Upon Unpublished
    Letters 1807–1824* (London, 1939).
Wordsworth, William, 'Letter', probably to Henry Crabbe Robinson
    (?1820), in *Byron: The Critical Heritage*, ed. A. Rutherford
    (London, 1970).

Further reading

Oscar José Santucho's *Lord Byron: A Comprehensive Bibliography
of Secondary Materials in English, 1807–1974* (Scarecrow Author
Bibliographies No. 30, New Jersey, 1977) is complete on *Don Juan*
up to 1974. It also lists imitations, continuations and forgeries of the
poem. In the Byron section of *The English Romantic Poets: A Review
of Research and Criticism*, ed. Frank Jordan (The Modern Language
Association of America, New York, 4th ed., 1985), John Clubbe
provides a judicious and excellent review of *Don Juan* criticism up to
1983, to which this writer is much indebted. A valuable selection of
nineteenth-century commentary on *Don Juan* is assembled in *Byron:
The Critical Heritage*, ed. Andrew Rutherford (London, 1970). A
good deal of material relevant to *Don Juan* is now usefully collected
in *Lord Byron: The Complete Miscellaneous Prose*, ed. A. Nicholson
(Oxford, 1991).

The making of *Don Juan*

J. M. Smeed's *Don Juan: Variations on a Theme* (London, 1990)
gives an account of the historical development of the Don Juan legend.
Oscar Mandel's *The Theatre of Don Juan: A Collection of Plays
and Views, 1630–1963* (London, 1963) remains useful.

    For an account of the composition of *Don Juan*, including Byron's
revisions, deletions and additions, the four volumes of Truman Guy

Steffan and Willis W. Pratt's *Byron's Don Juan: The Making of a Masterpiece* (1957, rev. Austin, Texas, 1971) remain invaluable. They are supplemented (and occasionally corrected) by the notes and commentary attached to Jerome J. McGann's Clarendon Press edition of the poem (Oxford, 1986). In *Keats-Shelley Journal*, 25 (1976), Leslie Marchand writes illuminatingly about 'Narrator and Narration in *Don Juan*'.

Sharply differing views of Byron's politics are presented by Malcolm Kelsall, *Byron's Politics* (London, 1987), and by Michael Foot, *The Politics of Paradise: A Vindication of Byron* (London, 1988). Carl Woodring's *Politics in English Romantic Poetry* (London, 1970) remains excellent on the political circumstances and events of the period as they affected Byron and other poets. Cecil Lang's 'Narcissus Jilted: Byron, *Don Juan*, and the Biographical Imperative', in *Historical Studies and Literary Criticism*, ed. Jerome J. McGann (Wisconsin, 1985) is provocative and stimulating. Leslie Marchand's three-volume *Byron: A Biography* (New York, 1957), and his later one-volume abridgement, *Byron: A Portrait* (New York, 1970), the latter containing some new material, are essential reading, as is Marchand's twelve-volume edition of the letters and journals (London, 1973–82), for anyone setting out to locate *Don Juan* within the context of its author's life and times.

Style and form

For the Italian background to Byron's poem, see A. D. Waller's long and informative introduction to his edition of Frere's *The Monks and the Giants* (see above); Peter Vassallo's *Byron: The Italian Literary Influence* (London, 1984); Giorgio Melchiori's 1958 Nottingham Byron Lecture, *Byron and Italy*; and Elizabeth French Boyd, *Byron's Don Juan: A Critical Study* (London, 1945). Boyd's book is still unrivalled for its wide-ranging account of the books Byron owned, his reading, and the great variety of literary influences, ancient and modern, English and French, as well as Italian, revealed by the poem. For the specifically British literary background, see A. B. England's *Byron's Don Juan and Eighteenth-Century Literature: A Study of Some Rhetorical Continuities and Discontinuities* (London, 1975), as well as Peter Graham's *Don Juan and Regency England* (Charlottesville, 1990), and the essays by Beatty, Gassenmeier, and Cooke in *Byron: Augustan and Romantic* (see above).

Rachel Brownstein, 'Byron's *Don Juan*: Some Reasons for the Rhymes' (*Modern Language Quarterly*, 28, 1967), is interesting on the comic rhymes, as are Peter Manning on '*Don Juan* and Byron's Imperceptiveness to the English Word', in *Studies in Romanticism*, 18 (2), 1979, and Peter Porter, 'Byron and the Moral North: The

Englishness of *Don Juan*', in *Encounter*, 43 (1974). Ronald Bottrall's 'Byron and the English Colloquial Tradition' (rpt. in *The English Romantic Poets*, ed. M. H. Abrams; Oxford, 1960) remains valuable, as do Alvin Kernan's chapter on *Don Juan* in *The Plot of Satire* (New Haven, 1965) and George Ridenour's *The Style of Don Juan* (New Haven, 1969).

The poem

The pre-eminence of *Don Juan* among Byron's works is reflected in the sheer volume of criticism devoted to it in this century. Everything written about the poem by its most recent editor, Jerome McGann, is worth reading: notably, *Don Juan in Context* (London, 1976); the relevant section in *Fiery Dust: Byron's Poetic Development* (London, 1968); 'The Book of Byron and the Book of a World', in his *The Beauty of Inflections: Literary Investigations in Historical Method and Theory* (Oxford, 1985); and the essay 'Byron, Mobility, and the Poetics of Historical Ventriloquism', in *Romanticism Past and Present*, 9 (1), 1985. In addition to works already cited, other critical books containing important accounts or insights about *Don Juan* include: M. K. Joseph, *Byron the Poet* (London, 1964); M. G. Cooke, *The Blind Man Traces the Circle: On the Patterns and Philosophy of Byron's Poetry* (London, 1969); Frederick L. Beaty, *Byron the Satirist* (Illinois, 1985); Peter Manning, *Byron and His Fictions* (Detroit, 1978); Paul Trueblood, *The Flowering of Byron's Genius: Studies in Byron's Don Juan* (Stanford, California, 1945); and the section on the poem in Alvin Kernan's *The Plot of Satire* (New Haven, 1965). In ' "Words Are Things": Byron and the Prophetic Efficacy of Language' (*Studies in English Literature 1500–1900*, 25, Autumn 1985), L. E. Marshall writes well about Byron's artistic search 'to find the place where words and things cohere'. Byron's intelligent and individual treatment of the poem's heroines receives long overdue attention in Susan J. Wolfson's ' "Their She Condition": Cross-Dressing and the Politics of Gender in *Don Juan*', in *English Literary History*, 54 (3), 1987, and in Carolyn Franklin's *Byron's Heroines* (Oxford, 1992).

The after-life of *Don Juan*

Clubbe's bibliography (see above) is extremely helpful in this area, as is the Appendix to vol. IV of Steffan and Pratt's *Byron's Don Juan: The Making of A Masterpiece* which deals with the poem's reception and influence in England, America and Europe. P. G. Trueblood's symposium, *Byron's Political and Cultural Influence in Nineteenth-Century Europe* (London, 1981) assembles a good deal of material, as does *Lord Byron and His Contemporaries*, ed. C.E. Robinson (London, 1982). S.C. Chew's *Byron In England* (cited above) remains useful. D.E. Erdman in 'Byron and Revolt in England', in *Science and Society*, 11 (1947), 'Byron and the Genteel Reformers', in *PMLA*, 56 (1941) and 'Byron and the New Force of the People', in *The Keats-Shelley Journal*, 11 (1962) discusses the political and social influence of *Don Juan*. See also, William Leonard, *Byron and Byronism in America* (Boston, 1969), Keith Walker, *Byron's Readers: A Study of Attitudes Towards Byron 1812–1832* (Salzburg Studies in English Literature, Salzburg, 1979), Jay A. Ward, *The Critical Reputation of Byron's Don Juan in Britain* (Salzburg, 1979), Charles J. Clancy, *Review of Don Juan Criticism 1900–1973* (1974) and the papers delivered at the 1978 Byron Symposium in Constance, ed. R. Schowerling. *The Byron Journal* 1973– is characterized by an interest in Byron's influence outside England.

For more specialized studies, see John Bayley's 'Pushkin and Byron', in *The Byron Journal*, 16 (1988), and the relevant section in Bayley's *Pushkin: A Comparative Commentary* (Cambridge, 1971), as well as S.S. Hoisington, *Eugene Onegin: An Inverted Byron Poem*, in *Comparative Literature*, 17 (1975), and David Matual, 'Chekhov's "Black Monk" and Byron's "Black Friar" ', in *International Fiction Review* (1978). Grabbe's use of *Don Juan* and *The Deformed Transformed* is discussed by the present writer in Rutherford's *Byron: Augustan and Romantic* (cited above). Edmond Estève's *Byron et le Romantisme français* (Paris, 1907) remains authoritative. B.J. Tysdahl writes about 'Byron, Norway, and Ibsen's *Peer Gynt*' in *English Studies*, 56 (1975). Edward Fiess discusses 'Melville as a Reader and Student of Byron', in *American Literature*, 24 (1952).